To the Father of All Grace,
the Son of His Love,
and the Spirit of His Joy;

Thank You for sharing Your consuming love,
Your extravagant goodness,
Your exhilarating joy,
Your radiant glory,
And Your abundant life with us.

We are Yours forever.

Unless otherwise stated, English definitions of Greek and Hebrew words are taken from the *HELPS Lexicon* as published within *The Discovery Bible* software, available at thediscoverybible.com.

Unless otherwise stated, all Scripture quotations are taken from *The ESV Bible* (The Holy Bible, English Standard Version), copyright © 2001 by Crossway, a publishing ministry of Good News Publishers. Used by permission. All rights reserved.

Scripture quotations marked (NASB) are taken from *The New American Standard Bible* ® (1995 Update) Copyright ©1960, 1962, 1963, 1968, 1971, 1972, 1973, 1975, 1977, 1995 by the Lockman Foundation. Used by permission. All rights reserved.

Scripture quotations marked (NKJV) are taken from *The New King James Version*, ©1979, 1980, 1982 by Thomas Nelson, Inc. Used by permission. All rights reserved.

Scripture quotations marked (BSB) are taken from *The Berean Study Bible New Testament,* copyright © 2016, Bible Hub (Biblehub.com). Used by permission. All rights reserved.

Scripture quotations marked (NLT) are taken from the *Holy Bible: New Living Translation*. Wheaton, Ill: Tyndale House Publishers, copyright © 2004. Used by permission. All rights reserved.

Scripture quotations marked (TDB) are taken from *The Discovery Bible,* copyright © 2018, HELPS Ministries Inc. Used by permission. All rights reserved.

Scripture quotations marked (NRSV) are taken from *The Holy Bible: New Revised Standard Version*. 1989. Nashville: Thomas Nelson Publishers.

Thanks to Brian Upsher for editorial support, Nikki Miller and Donna Nichol for proofing. And of course, thanks to my wife Melanie, without whom this book would not have been possible.

And He Will by Geoff Woodcock
Book Three of the *One with Christ Series*
Revision 2, January 2021

ISBN: 978-0-9951408-3-7
ISSN: 2624-411X
Published by Acacia Media | www.acacia.media
Printed in the United States of America

Other Formats
978-0-9951408-6-8 (PDF)
978-0-9951408-4-4 (Kindle)
978-0-9951408-5-1 (ePub)

This book is available free online at www.onewithchrist.org

© 2020, Geoff Woodcock. Freely receive, freely give.

Anyone may freely print, copy, reproduce, store, and distribute this book for non-commercial purposes. If you would like to reproduce this book for profit or for charitable fundraising, please make a request by emailing: support@acacia.media.

AND HE WILL

Geoff Woodcock

onewithchrist.org

Contents

Introduction i

COVENANT

1. Seek First the Kingdom 1
2. Kingdom Within 7
3. Covenant of Blood 13
4. For Jesus 20
5. The Exchange 27
6. Eternal Life 34
7. Stages of Covenant 42

SPIRIT AND FLESH

8. The Flesh 47
9. Identity 54
10. Circumcising the Heart 61
11. No Other Saviour 68
12. Everything Already 75
13. Waves Rise Up 82
14. Not I but Christ 89
15. Set Apart 95
16. Righteous Judgment 101
17. Immersed in Fire 107

18 . Judgment and Design 113
19 . Renewing the Mind.. 120
20 . Blessing or Curse? 127
21 . The Fight of Faith.. 135
22 . All Authority... 143
23 . Overpowering Principalities................................. 151
24 . Journey of Love... 159
25 . Into the Land.. 165
26 . Choose Life... 172

Final Words 179

Connect 181

Small Groups 183

Study Guide 188

About the Author.. 220

Reference Notes... 221

Introduction

Daniel 12:3
And those who are wise shall shine
  like the brightness of the sky above;
  and those who turn many to righteousness,
  like the stars forever and ever.

My daughter Keziah once performed a science experiment about the states of matter. In school, everyone learns about solids, liquids and gases. When water is in its solid state, it is known as *ice*. As a liquid we call it *water*, and when it is a gas, we call it *steam*. Because we do not usually see gases, we pay them little attention, even though our very life depends on the air we breathe. Most of the time, we only think about the solids and liquids because they are what we can taste, touch and see.

Keziah's project was not focused on solids, liquids or gases. Her goal was to make plasma—a state that exists beyond gas. Plasma is created when a gas becomes charged with energy. We see plasma in lightning, in the sun, and in the stars. It is a state of energy and light that makes up 99.9% of the visible universe. And yet few people give it any thought.

Matthew 22:35-39
And one of them, a lawyer, asked him a question to test him. "Teacher, which is the great commandment in the Law?" And he said to him, "You shall love the Lord your God with all your heart and with all your soul and with all your mind. This is the great and first commandment. And a second is like it: You shall love your neighbour as yourself."

Like plasma, here Jesus describes a state of life that few people know even exists. It is a state of wholehearted love, where the love of God so consumes us and the power of His Spirit so energises us that we become people who radiate the glory of God. This is a life where the light of God's love shines through us and we stand out like stars in the darkness of a selfish world.

But is this kind of life really possible?

> **Ephesians 3:20**
> Now to him who is able to do far more abundantly than all that we ask or think, according to the power at work within us...

God is awesome in power and in love, and He can do abundantly more than we could ever imagine. For as the Amplified version reads: God is able to do "superabundantly, far over and above all that we dare ask or think, infinitely beyond our highest prayers, desires, thoughts, hopes, or dreams." All things are equally effortless for the Living God, and He can easily empower us to love Him with all our heart, soul, mind, and strength. If God has commanded it, He can do it.

Knowing that God has the power and desire to surpass our dreams, let us dream! Can we imagine a life so immersed in God's presence that His love radiates out of every part of us? God can take us beyond that. Can we imagine living in such close union with Him that people look into our eyes and see the fire of His love? God can do it. Can we imagine the power of God flowing through us and devastating the darkness, bringing His light and love to the world? He can surpass even that. God can do far more than we can imagine or dream, and He wants to do it. He has the vision. All He seeks is our agreement and devotion.

> **Jeremiah 33:9** (BSB)
> "So this city will bring Me renown, joy, praise, and glory before all the nations of the earth, who will hear of all the good I do for it. They will tremble in awe because of all the goodness and prosperity I will provide it."

John 10:10
"The thief comes only to steal and kill and destroy. I came that they may have life and have it abundantly."

Scripture gives us insight into the abundant life that Jesus longs to give us— a life of wholehearted love, deep intimacy, inexpressible joy, perfect peace, complete freedom, unshakeable hope, and extravagant blessing. In fact, God wants to reveal so much of His goodness through us that the people of the world look at us in awe. *How can they have such peace in times of such stress? Why are they so joyful? What is that light in their eyes? Where did they find such love?* This is the spiritual prosperity that God has prepared for us. But do we share His vision? Do we have the faith and hunger to pursue a life of wholehearted love?

Faith and Desire

Isaiah 1:19 (BSB)
If you are willing and obedient, you will eat the best of the land.

If we are willing and obedient, we will enjoy the best life that God has for us. But what if we do not share God's desire for our life and are not truly willing to commit to His will? If this is the case, we need to be honest with God. He can take it; in fact He wants it. So even if we have only a flickering flame of desire for God, we can present what we have to God and ask Him to increase it. God longs for us to enjoy an awesome zeal for Him, so He will never snuff out the smouldering wick—He will meet us where we are and nourish our desire until we share His passion for love and unity with Jesus.[1] If we are willing to be willing, He will do the rest.

Desire always works with faith, and faith comes by hearing the voice of God. So, I would like to encourage you to take time to connect with the Holy Spirit as you read this book. Listen for His voice and ask Him to share His desires with you. If you do not sense the life of the Spirit as you read, or if the book is dry and hard to understand, then leave it for a while. Focus on what God is doing now and come back to this book later.

If the Spirit breathes life into these pages as you read, then enjoy them! Open your heart to receive faith and then pursue and possess the inheritance that God has prepared for you. If you encounter some things that are difficult to believe at first, take it to the Holy Spirit. It is His job to lead us into truth and reality. Do not be like some of the disciples who turned away from Jesus when His words were hard to accept.[2] Instead, test what you read by working it through with the Spirit and the word of God. Let the Holy Spirit show you what is true and then ask Him to make His truth your reality.

And He Will

This is the third book in the *One with Christ* series. For readers who have not read the previous books, key material is briefly summarised as needed. Like the previous books, at the end of this book is a Study Guide with a set of exercises for each chapter. These are designed to help you connect to Jesus and give His Spirit space to speak to you. I am sure that the encounters you will have with God as you do them will be both precious and transforming.

This whole book is based on the belief that God will keep His promises. *And He Will* is not just a title, but a statement of faith and practice. Keep this in mind as you read this book. All the chapters focus on God's promises and how He fulfils them. Please do not be tempted to make anything happen in your own strength. After all, can you make yourself love God with all your heart and soul? No? Then give up on yourself now and put your trust in God. Wholehearted love is something that only God can do, and He has promised to do it! We simply need to give Him our permission to make it a reality.

This book is structured like a journey. In the first section called "Covenant," we look at our goal: a life of wholehearted love. We discover how this life is found in unity with Jesus and how Jesus makes unity with Him possible through covenant. In the second section, "Spirit and Flesh," we look at how Jesus makes the cross real in our lives by baptising us into His death and removing the selfishness from our hearts. We discover how this death of self and selfishness is essential to living a life of selfless, wholehearted love with Jesus. In "Fight for Life," we then look at the nature of our new life with Christ and God's design for our lives in relationship to others. We also explore our call to keep overcoming the enemy and to keep growing in Christ.

As you read, I pray that God would enlighten the eyes of your understanding and grant you wisdom and revelation in His love and glory. May you enter the fullness of His inheritance for you—the riches of the life and freedom that is found in Jesus Christ.

Geoff (Jeff) Woodcock

PART ONE | COVENANT

1 | Seek First the Kingdom

> **Matthew 6:33**
> "But seek first the kingdom of God and his righteousness, and all these things will be added to you."

If we are to follow Jesus, then our first priority must be to seek the kingdom of God. When we seek the kingdom and the righteousness of Christ, Jesus guarantees to provide everything we need in this life. But is Jesus speaking these words to us? Are all believers already a part of the kingdom of God? If so, then why should we seek a kingdom that we already possess?

Before we look at these questions, we need to understand what the kingdom of God is and how we possess the kingdom. In the natural realm, the term *kingdom* describes everything that is under the rule of a king or queen. Without a king or queen, there can be no kingdom. In the same way, the kingdom of God only exists because Jesus is the King of kings.

The Gift of the Kingdom

> **Luke 12:32**
> "Fear not, little flock, for it is your Father's good pleasure to give you the kingdom."

The Father delights to give us the kingdom of God. Like all of God's gifts, the kingdom is a gift that is received through relationship. For example, we receive the gift of redemption when we come to know Jesus as our Redeemer. Likewise, we receive the gift of salvation when we come to know Jesus as our Saviour. The call to seek the kingdom of God is therefore first and foremost a call to relationship: it is an invitation to personally know Jesus as our king.

Because knowing Jesus as our king is a gift, we cannot earn or even believe our way into the kingdom. It is a gift that we can only receive by faith.

I once visited a friend and noticed a toy jewel on the table. It was glass and shaped like a very large diamond. We started to talk about the gifts of God and how often we can feel like we need to earn God's blessings. I gave him the jewel as a token of the gifts of God and said, "Take this jewel. Now pretend you're God and you want to give it to me as a blessing." His eyes lit up.

"Hey Geoff, you know, I really love you and I want to give you this precious jewel as a blessing to show you how much I love you." I reached out for the jewel and responded.

"Thank you! I would love that blessing! I'll give you $1 for it." He looked surprised.

"No, you don't understand. It's a gift of my love. It's completely free. I just want to bless you with it. Take it. It's yours. I love you!"

"Thank you so much! I love you too! Here, I'll give you $2 for it."

A mixture of confusion and frustration came over his face. It was impossible to put a price on a priceless gift, and if he sold it to me, it would no longer be a gift. This meant we were at an impasse. He genuinely wanted to bless me, and I wanted to be blessed. But because I kept trying to pay for the blessing, he was unable to give it to me.

This exact principle exists within the kingdom of God. As soon as we try to earn our way into the kingdom, we prevent God from giving it to us as a free gift. This robs Him of the pleasure He receives in giving us the kingdom. Therefore, as we set out to seek the kingdom, we need to repent from trying to earn anything from God. Every instinct to make ourselves good enough for God's blessing must completely die. When we accept that we can never earn the kingdom, we become free to receive it through faith as a blessing of God's extravagant, unconditional love.

A Kingdom Inheritance

James 2:5
Listen, my beloved brothers, has not God chosen those who are poor in the world to be rich in faith and heirs of the kingdom, which he has promised to those who love him?

Through faith we become heirs or inheritors of the kingdom. Because God gives us the kingdom as an inheritance, there is a process that we must go through before we can personally possess the kingdom. We can see this principle in the natural realm. Imagine we were given the gift of citizenship of another country. We did not earn it, nor did we deserve it. We simply received the offer. Yet, that gift would make no difference to us unless we were first willing to give up our current citizenship and relocate to the new land. Only then would we know all the blessings and privileges that come with being a citizen of this new country. The same is true for the kingdom of God. If we are to seek first the kingdom, we need to be prepared for change.

Matthew 6:9-10
"Pray then like this:
'Our Father in heaven,
hallowed be your name.
Your kingdom come,
your will be done,
on earth as it is in heaven.'"

Matthew 7:21
"Not everyone who says to me, 'Lord, Lord,' will enter the kingdom of heaven, but the one who does the will of my Father who is in heaven."

Your kingdom come; Your will be done.
In *Bride Arise,* we learned that every dimension of relationship with God requires something of us.[1] If we want to know God as our Father, we need to stop trying to earn His affection and just let Him embrace us. If we want to know Jesus as our Teacher, we need to prepare our hearts like good soil to

receive the seed of His word. If we want to know Jesus as our Bridegroom, we need to make an exclusive covenant of love with Jesus. All these unique relationships are available to us as part of our inheritance in Christ. Yet each one requires something of us.

This principle is especially true for knowing Jesus as our king. From the very beginning of our spiritual journey, we are taught to call Jesus our *Lord*. We use the word so often that it can be easy to lose sight of its real meaning. The terms *Lord* and *King* both speak of a relationship in which God rules over us and we obey His will. In this sense, becoming a citizen of the kingdom of God means accepting a change in government. We must give up all rights to govern our own lives and embrace a life of faith-based obedience. This is why Jesus teaches us to pray for the kingdom of God to come *and* His will be done. The only way to know Jesus as our personal king is to first abandon the throne of our lives and take our place as His subjects. *Your will be done.*

This brings us back to our original question: Are all believers already a part of the kingdom of God? The answer is found in another question: Do all believers actively obey the will of God? Sadly, no. So many of us still seek our own will instead of God's will and so forfeit the blessings of the kingdom life. For this reason, God is calling us all to seek first the kingdom of God.

The Beginning of Obedience

The kingship of Christ requires our obedience and in any sphere of life, obedience begins with the most important tasks. Employees do not receive praise for doing tasks 6-10 if they neglect tasks 1-5, neither are soldiers commended for cleaning their uniforms if they ignore the command to engage the enemy. In the same way, we cannot think that we are obedient to God if we only keep the lesser commands. Our obedience needs to begin with the greatest, most important commands.

> **Matthew 22:35-40 (BSB)**
> One of them, an expert in the law, tested Him with a question: "Teacher, which commandment is the greatest in the Law?"

> Jesus declared, "'Love the Lord your God with all your heart and with all your soul and with all your mind. This is the first and greatest commandment. And the second is like it: 'Love your neighbour as yourself.' All the Law and the Prophets hang on these two commandments."

In this passage, Jesus reveals His highest will for our lives. The whole of Scripture hangs on these commands and the entire will of God is found in them. These commands of love are God's royal law for all those in His kingdom. Yet this law is not like legalism, which uses the fear of punishment and the promise of reward to control our behaviour. Rather, this is the perfect law of Spirit, life and liberty. It is the law of profound peace and unshakeable joy. It is Christ's reign of love, given to set us truly free!

Therefore, by calling us to seek first the kingdom, Jesus is not wanting us to learn a theology but to live a life. He is calling us to make the first command our first priority; to seek first the reality of loving God with our entire being, and then let His love flow through us to others.

And those who seek shall find. It is the Father's good pleasure to give us the kingdom and so if we invest our all in seeking the kingdom, we can be sure that we will possess it. Jesus Himself will share His heart with us, put His Spirit in us, and empower us to live a life of wholehearted love.

Like a Child

> **Mark 10:13-16**
>
> And they were bringing children to him that he might touch them, and the disciples rebuked them. But when Jesus saw it, he was indignant and said to them, "Let the children come to me; do not hinder them, for to such belongs the kingdom of God. Truly, I say to you, whoever does not receive the kingdom of God like a child shall not enter it." And he took them in his arms and blessed them, laying his hands on them.

The only way to receive the kingdom is like a child: full of faith and humility. Children have nothing to lose and are comfortable living in dependence, so they take Jesus at His word. They think that when Jesus says love is the greatest command, it must be the greatest command. It is usually adults who argue against the design of wholehearted love. They are quick to cite obscure Scriptures and complex theologies to explain away love. But children have a beautiful simplicity. When they hear the call to seek first the kingdom, they respond by seeking first the kingdom. When they hear God's promise to make it possible, they believe Him. They think, *God is God, He can do what He has promised.*

Let us start to believe like little children. Let us believe that what Jesus says is true and accept His call to a life of selfless love. Let us seek first His kingdom!

Pray

Father, thank you for the gift of the Kingdom. Thank you for the gift of Jesus. I would like to know Him as my king. Please remove everything from my life that would resist His reign of love. Jesus, I submit to you and I give you the throne of my heart. Let your will be done!

2 | Kingdom Within

> **Luke 17:20-21** (NKJV)
> Now when He was asked by the Pharisees when the kingdom of God would come, He answered them and said, "The kingdom of God does not come with observation; nor will they say, 'See here!' or 'See there!' For indeed, the kingdom of God is within you."

The Greek word *entos*, which is translated as *within*, can also be translated as *in the midst* or *among*. From either perspective the verse remains true. The Pharisees of Jesus' time believed that the Messiah would establish a physical kingdom and set free Israel from foreign rule. They continually looked for outward signs that would signal the coming of the kingdom. Yet the kingdom was in their midst—not in palaces, throne-rooms or fortresses, but in the person of Jesus Christ. He is both king and kingdom.

> **Colossians 1:24-27**
> Now I rejoice in my sufferings for your sake, and in my flesh I am filling up what is lacking in Christ's afflictions for the sake of his body, that is, the church, of which I became a minister according to the stewardship from God that was given to me for you, to make the word of God fully known, the mystery hidden for ages and generations but now revealed to his saints. To them God chose to make known how great among the Gentiles are the riches of the glory of this mystery, which is Christ in you, the hope of glory.

This is a mystery of great glory: **Jesus lives in us**. When we are filled with the Spirit of Jesus, we possess the King of all creation and so His kingdom is truly found within us. Our hearts become His throne-room and our bodies become His temple.

Bought with a Price

> 1 Corinthians 6:15-20 (emphasis added)
> Do you not know that your bodies are members of Christ? Shall I then take the members of Christ and make them members of a prostitute? Never! Or do you not know that he who is joined to a prostitute becomes one body with her? For, as it is written, "The two will become one flesh." But **he who is joined to the Lord becomes one spirit with him**. Flee from sexual immorality. Every other sin a person commits is outside the body, but the sexually immoral person sins against his own body. Or do you not know that your body is a temple of the Holy Spirit within you, whom you have from God? **You are not your own, for you were bought with a price.** So glorify God in your body.

"He who is joined to the Lord becomes one spirit with him." Unity with Jesus exists at the heart of the kingdom of God. As we learned in *First Love*, when we are joined to Christ, we become one spirit with Him and this unity enables us to share His heart and mind. It does not mean we become God. But it does mean that we can experience the feelings and the thoughts of Christ as He shares them with us.

> Ezekiel 36:26-27
> And I will give you a new heart, and a new spirit I will put within you. And I will remove the heart of stone from your flesh and give you a heart of flesh. And I will put my Spirit within you, and cause you to walk in my statutes and be careful to obey my rules.

In this verse we see the awesome grace of God in action. God gives us a new heart and puts His Spirit in us *so that* we can keep His commands. God does not expect us to obey Him in our own strength. He knows that we can never make ourselves love Him with all our heart and soul. The only way we can keep the first command is to let the Spirit of Jesus love through us with all His heart and soul. All we need to do is stop trying so hard and instead, surrender ourselves to becoming one with Christ. He will do the rest.

"You are not your own, for you were bought with a price." Our relationship with Jesus as our king is one of mutual possession. We possess the kingdom by receiving it as a gift from the Father. However, we were purchased with a price. Like the man who found the treasure in a field, or the pearl merchant who sold everything he had to buy the pearl of great value, Jesus gave His life—everything He had—to purchase us. Jesus bought us with His blood to be His possession, and now He owns everything we are and everything we have. In this sense, we only truly possess the kingdom when we are possessed by the King.

So what does a life look like when it is possessed by Christ?

Many of us know what it is like to be possessed. There was a time when I was in a dark place and I allowed a spirit of rage to enter my life. At one point, the anger was so intense that I picked up a person with what seemed like superhuman strength and ejected them from the room with stunning speed. I understood how easily the demon-possessed man could have beaten the seven sons of Sceva.[1] The people watching me were shocked and I was ashamed. I was completely out of control.

If a demon of rage can give someone superhuman strength and make them act in uncontrollable anger, what would it look like for the Spirit of Jesus to possess us? Surely it can only mean being filled with a supernatural zeal that compels us to act with extreme, selfless love. This extravagant love must be the evidence that Jesus is truly alive within us.

This leaves me to wonder if there is a difference between being filled with the Spirit and being possessed by the Spirit. Like the disciples, we can receive the Holy Spirit when Jesus breathes upon us, but still lack the power from on high. We can operate in the spiritual gifts, have faith to move mountains, prophesy all things, and yet still lack His love. To be possessed by the Spirit of Jesus requires something more of us than superficial surrender. It calls for us to abandon all rights to our lives and accept that we were bought at a price and we are not our own. We belong to God as a life for His possession.

> [The Holy Spirit] is a person, with all the faculties of a Person, exactly like the Saviour. He has intelligence, love, and a will of His own; and as a Person, before He comes to live in a man, He must be given full possession of His body… He must come and dwell in flesh and blood.
> …But He [God] showed us, "There is all the difference in the world between *your* surrendered life in My hands, and Me living *My* life in your body."
>
> - Norman Grubb, recounting the words of Rees Howells[2]

It is one thing for the Spirit of Jesus to live *in* us and something else entirely for Christ to live *through* us. When we invite Jesus to take possession of us and to live His life through us, we give Him everything we are and everything we have to be used for His love.

One day I thought of my pet dog, Sasha. I own her. She has a kennel, a collar, a mat, and a bowl. And she thinks they are hers. But she belongs to me and I own everything she has. Her sense of ownership is an illusion. It is the same for us. If we belong to God, then everything that we think is ours actually belongs to Him. This truth became clear to me one day when I asked the Lord, "What have you given me to give away?"

"The blue car. Give it to Miles." God replied instantly and I flinched a little. I loved that car. It was a miracle of God's goodness that we came to own it. This was the only car I ever found to be a true joy to drive. And now I had to let it go.

I asked my wife Melanie to talk to God about it and she asked Him for a clear confirmation. Within hours, a friend came round to our house and met her at the door.

"Guess what I did today?" he said. "I gave away a car." He had no idea what we were seeking God about. Then Melanie opened the Scriptures and continued reading through Acts. She picked up her reading at the verse which says that "no one counted anything as their own."[3] She told me about the confirmations, and we gave the car away. In a single act, the car became a vehicle of God's love and joy. Miles was overwhelmed with thankfulness and praised God as he drove home. He then shared about the extravagant love of God with many people in his neighbourhood who were curious to hear the story. The spiritual fruit of the gift was worth vastly more than the value of any car.

I was also deeply thankful for the fruit in my own life. It is easy to love when our giving is convenient and does not involve any real loss or cost. But sacrificial love brings an integrity to the soul that cannot come any other way. This one simple act blessed me with a sense of integrity and an increased capacity in my heart that has never left me. Only when we see the fruit of our actions do we realise that there is no real cost to love. Every loving sacrifice is an investment that always brings a return.

All Needs Provided

Matthew 6:25-33

"Therefore I tell you, do not be anxious about your life, what you will eat or what you will drink, nor about your body, what you will put on. Is not life more than food, and the body more than clothing? Look at the birds of the air: they neither sow nor reap nor gather into barns, and yet your heavenly Father feeds them. Are you not of more value than they? And which of you by being anxious can add a single hour to his span of life? And why are you anxious about clothing? Consider the lilies of the field, how they grow: they neither toil nor spin, yet I tell you, even Solomon in all his glory was not arrayed like one of these. But if God so clothes the grass of the field, which today is alive and tomorrow is thrown into the oven, will he not much more clothe you, O you of little faith? Therefore do not be anxious, saying, 'What shall we eat?' or 'What shall we drink?' or 'What shall we wear?' For the Gentiles seek after all these things, and your heavenly Father knows that you need them all. But seek first the kingdom of God and his righteousness, and all these things will be added to you."

In this passage, Jesus promises to supply all the material needs we will ever have in this life. This promise of provision is not simply to sweeten the gospel message. Instead, Jesus promises to supply all our needs so that we can have the confidence to truly embrace a life of selfless love. We can pour out our lives without fear, knowing that even if Jesus leads us to give everything we have away in love, He will still take care of all our basic needs. He is our Shepherd, and He has guaranteed us that we shall lack nothing.

This kind of faith and dependence demands reality. We cannot trust in a theology to supply our needs. We can only trust in Jesus—the real and living God, who speaks to us, loves us, and will always take care of us. As we come to know Him as our King, our Possessor and our Provider, we will discover the joy and freedom of being His. We do not need to pursue wealth or secure our lives. Jesus has us in the palm of His hand. He loves us and He will never fail us.

Scripture says that we brought nothing into the world and can take nothing with us.[4] Everything of this life will pass away when we die. Then what are we left with? The only thing we can take into eternity is the capacity for love and unity with Jesus that we have forged in this life. If only we saw our lives in the light of eternity; if only we trusted in His unbreakable promise of provision, we would find ourselves set free to love extravagantly. This is our calling and it is worth the risk. Let us be possessed by the King of Love.

Pray

Jesus, I love you. Thank you for your promise of provision. Please burn it into my heart so that I can love freely without any thought for myself. Thank you that you are thinking of all my needs, all the time. You have it covered. I am excited about your will for me. Please help me to embrace a life of full obedience and wholehearted love. I give you permission to do whatever it takes to fulfil your vision for my life. Let your will be done!

3 | Covenant of Blood

Jesus often speaks of the kingdom of God in terms of a marriage. In the natural realm, all marriages are created through mutual agreement. If a person is forced into marriage it is not a true marriage at all. Every person must be free to choose love.

The kingdom of God is present where Christ reigns in love. Yet because love must always be a free gift, no one can be made to enter the kingdom. It has to be a willing choice, free from any manipulation or control. This means that the kingdom of God cannot advance through conquest. His reign of love only extends on the earth through agreement. *Let Your will be done.*

> **Hebrews 13:20-21**
> Now may the God of peace who brought again from the dead our Lord Jesus, the great shepherd of the sheep, by the blood of the eternal covenant, equip you with everything good that you may do his will, working in us that which is pleasing in his sight, through Jesus Christ, to whom be glory forever and ever. Amen.

When we come into relationship with God, we are brought into an eternal covenant with God through the blood of Jesus Christ. This covenant is not just the promise of salvation. It is the foundational agreement between God and us that defines our relationship and reveals what it means to live in His kingdom.

Our entire relationship with God takes place in the context of this covenant and so if we are to grow in Christ, we need to understand what it means to live in covenant with Him.

Covenants of Old

In ancient times, a covenant was a formal agreement that would unite people, families, villages or nations. In political situations, covenants were used in the form of treaties. The stronger nation would set out the terms of the covenant and the weaker nation was given the option of accepting those terms and living in peace or rejecting the covenant and risking war.

Within communities, covenants were often made to secure peace between families and to increase their defensive forces if attacked. In these cases, covenants were a matter of life and death—each group committed to risking their lives for the other in order to secure the same help when they needed it.

In the process of making a covenant, the families would negotiate until they reached terms they were willing to die for. Once an agreement was made, the parties would then sacrifice an animal and cut it in half. The blood would flow onto the ground as a silent witness to the new life being birthed through covenant. Both parties would then pass between the halves of the animal, walking through its blood, signifying that they were now bound together in the blood of one life. This was also a statement to those watching that each party was prepared to accept the penalty of death should they ever break the covenant. Having sealed the covenant in blood, the people would often eat and drink together like a family, in recognition of their unity and the new life they were now beginning.

A full treatment of the subject of covenant is far beyond the scope of this book. For now, we will briefly look at three key covenants in Scripture: God's covenant with Abraham, with Moses, and the new covenant through Jesus Christ.

God's Covenant with Abraham

Genesis 12:1-4a

Now the Lord said to Abram, "Go from your country and your kindred and your father's house to the land that I will show you. And I will make of you a great nation, and I will bless you and make your name great, so that you will be a blessing. I will bless those who bless you, and him who dishonours you I will curse, and in you all the families of the earth shall be blessed."

So Abram went, as the Lord had told him, and Lot went with him.

God's relationship with Abraham (Abram) began with a command and a promise. God called Abram to leave his homeland and move to Canaan. God promised to bless Abram and make him into a great nation, one in whom all the families of the earth would be blessed. Abram obeyed God and left in search of the country God had prepared for him.

Genesis 15:1-21 (NKJV)
After these things the word of the Lord came to Abram in a vision, saying, "Do not be afraid, Abram. I am your shield, your exceedingly great reward."

But Abram said, "Lord God, what will You give me, seeing I go childless, and the heir of my house is Eliezer of Damascus?" Then Abram said, "Look, You have given me no offspring; indeed one born in my house is my heir!"

And behold, the word of the Lord came to him, saying, "This one shall not be your heir, but one who will come from your own body shall be your heir." Then He brought him outside and said, "Look now toward heaven, and count the stars if you are able to number them." And He said to him, "So shall your descendants be."

And he believed in the LORD, and He accounted it to him for righteousness.

Then He said to him, "I am the LORD, who brought you out of Ur of the Chaldeans, to give you this land to inherit it."

And he said, "LORD GOD, how shall I know that I will inherit it?"

So He said to him, "Bring Me a three-year-old heifer, a three-year-old female goat, a three-year-old ram, a turtledove, and a young pigeon." Then he brought all these to Him and cut them in two, down the middle, and placed each piece opposite the other; but he did not cut the birds in two. And when the vultures came down on the carcasses, Abram drove them away.

As the sun was going down, a deep sleep fell on Abram. And behold, dreadful and great darkness fell upon him. Then the Lord said to Abram, "Know for certain that your offspring will be sojourners in a land that is not theirs and will be servants there, and they will be afflicted for four hundred years. But I will bring judgment on the nation that they serve, and afterward they shall come out with great possessions. As for you, you shall go to your fathers in peace; you shall be buried in a good old age. And they shall come back here in the fourth generation, for the iniquity of the Amorites is not yet complete."

And it came to pass, when the sun went down and it was dark, that behold, there appeared a smoking oven and a burning torch that passed between those pieces. On the same day the LORD made a covenant with Abram, saying:

"To your descendants I have given this land, from the river of Egypt to the great river, the River Euphrates— the Kenites, the Kenezzites, the Kadmonites, the Hittites, the Perizzites, the Rephaim, the Amorites, the Canaanites, the Girgashites, and the Jebusites."

God had promised to make Abram a great nation, yet Abram was old and childless. God therefore spoke to Abram and confirmed His promise. He then followed the ancient pattern and made a covenant with Abram. However, instead of having Abram walk through the blood with Him, God put Abram into a deep sleep. While he slept, a smoking firepot and a flaming torch passed between the pieces of the sacrifice, confirming God's covenant in blood. So what are the firepot and the flaming torch?

Scripture speaks of God as a consuming fire.[1] He is the fire in the burning bush and the pillar of fire in the wilderness. His presence burns with a fire of love that consumes the darkness. The smoking firepot is a symbol of God the Father.

Scripture speaks of salvation as a blazing torch and it refers to Jesus as the "source of eternal salvation."[2] Jesus is the Light of Revelation and the flaming torch of God.[3] Therefore, while Abram slept, Jesus passed between the pieces and made a covenant with the Father on behalf of Abraham.

Inheriting the Promises and the Blessings

Galatians 3:14-16

...so that in Christ Jesus the blessing of Abraham might come to the Gentiles, so that we might receive the promised Spirit through faith. To give a human example, brothers: even with a man-made covenant, no one annuls it or adds to it once it has been ratified. Now the promises were made to Abraham and to his offspring. It does not say, "And to offsprings," referring to many, but referring to one, "And to your offspring," who is Christ.

Because Jesus made a covenant with the Father on Abraham's behalf, all the promises that God made to Abraham ultimately belong to Jesus. The blessing of the Father belongs to Jesus. The land belongs to Jesus, the life belongs to Him, and the glory belongs to Him alone. Jesus then shares those blessings with His people. For as Scripture says: In Christ, we are blessed with every spiritual blessing.[4] In Christ, all the families of the earth are blessed.

Taking Responsibility

When Jesus made a covenant with the Father in our place, He not only inherited all the promises of the covenant, but He also took full responsibility for keeping all the demands of the covenant on our behalf. This means that we do not need to carry the burden of trying to obey God in our own strength. Instead, we can be yoked to Jesus and let Him obey God both for us and through us. *For us* means that because Jesus has already lived the perfect, righteous life and we live in union with Him, we can share His righteous standing before God. *Through us* means that if we are willing, Jesus will pour out the energising force of His love within us, which will make us want to act righteously.

But can we be sure Jesus wants to do this for us? Of course! Jesus delights to do the will of the Father and so He must be longing for the opportunity to obey the Father through us. And because it is only Jesus that makes our obedience possible, He alone receives all the glory for every righteous action we do. We remain simply vessels of His presence and love.

Bearing the Penalties
Jeremiah 34:18-20
"And the men who transgressed my covenant and did not keep the terms of the covenant that they made before me, I will make them like the calf that they cut in two and passed between its parts— the officials of Judah, the officials of Jerusalem, the eunuchs, the priests, and all the people of the land who passed between the parts of the calf. And I will give them into the hand of their enemies and into the hand of those who seek their lives. Their dead bodies shall be food for the birds of the air and the beasts of the earth."

In the reign of King Zedekiah, the people made a covenant with God to release the Hebrew slaves that they were holding captive. However, the people changed their mind and broke the covenant by keeping their fellow Hebrews in slavery. But they had passed between the pieces and had walked through the blood. They had bound themselves to life in covenant and to death outside covenant. So when they broke the covenant, there could only ever be one consequence: death.

When Jesus made a covenant with the Father on our behalf, He took both the burden and glory of our obedience. Yet He also took responsibility for our failure. At the very beginning, He knew as He walked through the blood that He would have to die because of our rebellion. And sure enough, we all chose our selfishness over God's love and failed to live according to His covenant design. And because of His commitment to the covenant, Jesus willingly paid the penalty and laid down His life for us.

At the cross, our failure was erased and death itself was defeated. Now we can enter into covenant with God through Jesus, forever free from the threat of death. As we stop striving in our own strength and learn to let Jesus live through us, we will find that He can easily bear the burden of our obedience. Through His Spirit, Jesus will empower us to live in covenant love.

Pray

Jesus, thank you for making a covenant with the Father on my behalf. Thank you for dying for me and for living in me. Please lead me deeper into a covenant life so that I may love you more.

4 | For Jesus

> **Matthew 26:26-29**
> While they were eating, Jesus took some bread, and after a blessing, He broke it and gave it to the disciples, and said, "Take, eat; this is My body." And when He had taken a cup and given thanks, He gave it to them, saying, "Drink from it, all of you; for this is My blood of the covenant, which is poured out for many for forgiveness of sins. But I say to you, I will not drink of this fruit of the vine from now on until that day when I drink it new with you in My Father's kingdom."

Here Jesus is making a covenant with His disciples. The wine is a symbol of Christ's blood, which Scripture calls the "blood of the eternal covenant."[1] Like the disciples, when we make a covenant with Jesus, we enter into a new life that starts now and lasts for all eternity.

Redemption and Forgiveness

> **Ephesians 1:7-8**
> In him we have redemption through his blood, the forgiveness of our trespasses, according to the riches of his grace, which he lavished upon us, in all wisdom and insight.

The blood of Jesus was poured out for the forgiveness of sins. In this passage, Paul connects redemption and forgiveness, both of which are legal terms. Redemption means to pay a ransom and forgiveness means to cancel a debt. At the cross, Jesus did both; He paid the ransom for our lives and He forgave our debt to God.[2]

But where did our debt come from?

Matthew 18:21-27
"Therefore the kingdom of heaven may be compared to a king who wished to settle accounts with his servants. When he began to settle, one was brought to him who owed him ten thousand talents. And since he could not pay, his master ordered him to be sold, with his wife and children and all that he had, and payment to be made. So the servant fell on his knees, imploring him, 'Have patience with me, and I will pay you everything.' And out of pity for him, the master of that servant released him and forgave him the debt."

In *Bride Arise,* we look at the parable of the unforgiving servant in terms of the debt that every person owes God. A debt is only created when there is a transfer of value. Therefore the servant in the parable owed the king ten thousand talents from the moment he borrowed the money, not from the time he lost the money. In the same way, we owe God a debt from the moment we are first born, not from the moment we first sin.

Our debt comes from the awesome value that God invested in us when He made us. In *First Love,* we look at this concept in terms of a clock. If we created a clock, it would owe us its existence from the moment it is created. It would repay the debt by living according to its design and telling us the time. That is where the clock's true value is found. It is the same for us: our debt stems from our design. Therefore, if we want to understand the nature of our debt and our value to God, we need to discover God's design for our lives.

Context of Love

John 17:24 (NASB, emphasis added)
"Father, I desire that they also, whom You have given Me, be with Me where I am, so that they may see My glory which You have given Me, **for You loved Me before the foundation of the world.**"

Here Jesus reveals the ultimate context of all creation. Before the world was ever created, the Father loved the Son. And long after this world ends, the Father will still love the Son. The love that flows between the Father and the

Son is the overarching reality that gives meaning to all creation—including us. God has created us entirely in the context of this flow of divine love.

> **Psalm 119:68**
> You are good and do good; teach me your statutes.

God always acts according to His nature and does what He is. God is good and does good. God is love and does love. So when God created us, He made us as creations of His love and goodness. No one came into being by chance or accident. No one was born for an ordinary life. On the contrary, God created every single person to be a living revelation of His love and goodness. *Especially you.*

For Jesus

> **Colossians 1:15-17**
> He [Jesus] is the image of the invisible God, the firstborn of all creation. For by him all things were created, in heaven and on earth, visible and invisible, whether thrones or dominions or rulers or authorities—all things were created through him and for him. And he is before all things, and in him all things hold together.

The Father created us through Jesus and *for* Jesus. God has wonderfully made each one of us to be a living gift of His love for Jesus. Jesus makes this clear in His final prayer:

> **John 17:25-26** (NASB, emphasis added)
> "O righteous Father, although the world has not known You, yet I have known You; and these have known that You sent Me; and I have made Your name known to them, and will make it known, **so that the love with which You loved Me may be in them, and I in them.**"

In His final prayer before the cross, Jesus speaks of making the Father known to us so that the Father's love for Jesus may live in us. In these words, Jesus reveals not only the greatest desire of His heart, but God's ultimate plan for humanity. **The Father designed us to be channels of His love for Jesus.** This is the reason for our creation. Every part of our being—spirit, heart, soul, mind and body—has been perfectly made to share the Father's love for Jesus.

So how much is the Father's love for Jesus worth? In the parable of the unforgiving servant, Jesus says the debt amounts to ten thousand talents. At the standard rate of pay, that amount would take a labourer 60 million days to earn. *60 million days.*

What Jesus is saying is that our value to God exceeds anything we could ever imagine. As channels of the love of God, from the moment of our conception, we take on the greatest value in all creation. This is because channels always take on the value of what flows through them. Electricity cables are valuable because of the power they carry. Rivers are valuable because of the water that flows in them. And we are valuable because we are created to flow with the Father's love for Jesus—the most valuable thing in all eternity.

However, like the servant in the parable, we all wasted our value. Instead of living in our design, we all chose to act in selfishness and block the flow of love. We denied Jesus the love that the Father wanted to flow through us and caused Him incredible loss. This created a debt that we could never repay.

Only when we see the extent of our debt to God do we realise how futile it is to try to earn our forgiveness. No one can work for 60 million days. No amount of good works will ever restore to Jesus the value of love that we stole from Him. All we can do is fall on our knees and ask for forgiveness. And as we receive God's forgiveness, our new life of love begins.

It is essential that we see the cross in the context of this divine design. So often we share about the cross as the place of forgiveness, but neglect to talk about *why* Jesus forgives us. We focus on the beginning and forget the end, not understanding that the saving power of God is set entirely within the context of God's design of love. Jesus forgives and redeems us in order to empower us to become channels of His Father's unfailing love. Love, not heaven, is the goal of salvation.

By Grace Through Faith

Ephesians 2:8-9
For by grace you have been saved through faith. And this is not your own doing; it is the gift of God, not a result of works, so that no one may boast.

Romans 5:1-2 (emphasis added)
Therefore, since we have been justified by faith, we have peace with God through our Lord Jesus Christ. Through him we have also obtained **access by faith** into this grace in which we stand, and we rejoice in hope of the glory of God.

Our covenant with God begins with forgiveness. In Chapter One, we saw how every blessing that God gives us is a free gift of His unconditional love. This includes forgiveness. Like an immeasurably precious jewel, forgiveness is a gift of God that cost Jesus His life and so is priceless beyond words. God can never sell us His forgiveness because then it would cease to be a gift. For this reason, Scripture says that we are saved by grace through faith. *By grace* means that salvation is a gift. *Through faith* means that we receive the gift with confidence in God's goodness, without trying to pay for it with our worthless works. We simply turn to God and put our trust in Him, and this gives the Holy Spirit permission to make His forgiveness a reality in our lives. As He does this, we experience the glorious feeling of being set free from all guilt, shame and condemnation.

Acts 26:15-18
"And I said, 'Who are You, Lord?' And the Lord said, 'I am Jesus whom you are persecuting. But get up and stand on your feet; for this purpose I have appeared to you, to appoint you a minister and a witness not only to the things which you have seen, but also to the things in which I will appear to you; rescuing you from the Jewish people and from the Gentiles, to whom I am sending you, to open their eyes so that they may turn from darkness to light and from the dominion of Satan to God, that they may receive forgiveness of sins and an inheritance among those who have been sanctified by faith in Me.'"

This process of faith to grace to reality is covered in previous *One with Christ* books in terms of inheritance and possession. When we receive the gift of forgiveness, God also gives us an inheritance that includes *every spiritual blessing in Christ*.[3] God holds nothing back, instead, it is like He gives us a million gifts, all wrapped in glistening foil. However, while we receive all these gifts the very moment we are born again, we do not experience them all at once. Instead, our present reality is made up of all the blessings that we have possessed through actual experience. Our inheritance speaks of the blessings to come; our possession speaks of the blessings we already have.

In order to enjoy the reality of each blessing, we need to take the time to unwrap and experience each one. And this requires *specific* faith. For example, before we can receive the gift of forgiveness, we need to have faith specifically for forgiveness. Do we want to receive salvation? We need faith for salvation. Do we want to discern God's voice? Then we need to believe that He speaks. Do we want to prophesy? We need faith for prophecy. Our whole spiritual journey depends on faith and this only comes from our ongoing relationship with the Holy Spirit. As it is written: The righteous shall live by faith.[4]

> **Romans 10:14-17**
> How then will they call on him in whom they have not believed? And how are they to believe in him of whom they have never heard? And how are they to hear without someone preaching? And how are they to preach unless they are sent? As it is written, "How beautiful are the feet of those who preach the good news!" But they have not all obeyed the gospel. For Isaiah says, "Lord, who has believed what he has heard from us?" So faith comes from hearing, and hearing through the word of Christ.

In *First Love*, we learn that faith is the heart-based confidence that comes from hearing God's voice. When the Holy Spirit speaks to us, He gives us the specific faith we need to access His grace, which then brings us into reality. By offering us both grace *and* faith, the Holy Spirit makes it His job to lead us into reality. He prohibits any works or self-generated effort on our part, as all striving comes from unbelief. In doing this, the Spirit removes any pressure we may feel to lead ourselves into reality. We can trust that He is more determined to make us a channel of love for Jesus than we could ever imagine. Our part is simply to take His hand and follow His lead into a life of love.

In the passage above, Paul writes of how we can work with the Holy Spirit to share this good news with the world. Our gospel is not merely a message of words, but one that is preached through our entire lives. As we allow Jesus to love the world through us, we can become a voice for His Spirit. Then, when we share His truth with a person, the Holy Spirit can anoint our words, speak through us, and impart to the hearer the faith for forgiveness. And then their journey into love can begin!

Pray

Father, thank you for making me a channel of your love for Jesus! Jesus, thank you for shedding your blood to forgive my debt. Father, please restore me to your design and share your love for Jesus with me. Let your love flow through every part of my being.

5 | The Exchange

When Jesus died on the cross, He offered everyone throughout history the gift of forgiveness. This is a gift He longs for everyone to accept. Why? Because the Father has created each person to share a unique measure of His love for Jesus. Both the Father and Son are absolutely committed to this design and will do whatever it takes to make it a reality. By offering everyone the gift of forgiveness, Jesus is inviting all people to take the first step into their design of love.

Reconciles and Makes Peace
> **Colossians 1:19-20a**
> For it was the Father's good pleasure for all the fullness to dwell in Him, and through Him to reconcile all things to Himself, having made peace through the blood of His cross…

The power of Jesus' blood does not end with forgiveness and redemption. In this passage, the blood of Jesus reconciles us to God. To reconcile is to restore a broken relationship and bring it back to a state of harmony. Through the blood of the cross, our sin is atoned for and our relationship with God is completely restored. By Christ's sacrifice, the fullness of every dimension of relationship with God is now available to us.

Cleanses
> **1 John 1:7**
> But if we walk in the Light as He Himself is in the Light, we have fellowship with one another, and the blood of Jesus His Son cleanses us from all sin.

To be forgiven is to be released from our debt and no longer held to account for our sin. As such, a person can be forgiven and free from the debt that their sin incurs, but not truly free from sin itself. Though forgiven, sin still lives within the person. In contrast, to be spiritually cleansed is to be washed clean from sin by its removal. Not only does the blood of Jesus secure our forgiveness, but it also washes away sin from our hearts, removing the pollution of sin and making us truly clean.

Justifies and Makes Righteous

> **Romans 5:9**
> Much more then, having now been justified by His blood, we shall be saved from the wrath of God through Him.

> **Justify / make righteous:** *dikaioo / dikaios* [1]
> To deem or show to be right, to be declared or pronounced righteous (by implication innocent).

We are both justified and made righteous through the blood of Christ. Justification is the ruling on the innocence of a person. As we drink the wine of His blood, Jesus takes us into unity with Him and shares His innocence with us.

> **Hebrews 10:16-17** [2]
> "This is the covenant that I will make with them after those days, says the LORD: I will put my laws upon their heart, and on their mind I will write them," He then says, "and their sins and their lawless deeds I will remember no more."

The blood of Jesus brings us into a place of spiritual innocence before God because it completely washes away our sin. Jesus takes our sin into His death and it is gone forever. God then permanently erases the memory of our sin. With all spiritual evidence of sin removed by the blood of Christ, we are perfectly innocent in the eyes, mind and heart of God.[3]

If we are to live in the reality of this innocence, we must first truly believe it. To do this, it is essential that we share God's forgetfulness concerning our sin. The enemy would seek to constantly remind us of our past sin because every time we recall our past sin, we disagree with God and choose unbelief over truth. We cannot allow our past sin to define us because it has all been completely erased by the blood of Christ. Instead, we are to let our union with Jesus define us and live in the glorious reality of being justified, righteous and perfectly innocent before Him.

Sanctifies

Hebrews 13:12
Therefore Jesus also, that He might sanctify the people through His own blood, suffered outside the gate.

Sanctify: *hagiazo*
To be set apart, to be made holy.

To be sanctified is to be set apart and made holy. Through the blood of Jesus, we are devoted to God and set apart from the world, sin and our fallen self. This setting apart is an inner, spiritual separation in which our hearts are disconnected from sin and connected to Jesus.

The word *hagiazo* comes from the word *hagios*, meaning *different*.[4] As the blood of Jesus makes us holy, our hearts are changed, and we become inherently different from the world and from our former lives. Jesus' blood reshapes the way we think, feel, act, desire and live. In this way, the sanctifying power of blood of Christ leads to true transformation.

Blood and Life

So why is the blood of Jesus so powerful? Why does His blood justify, sanctify, cleanse us, and make us holy?

> **Leviticus 17:11, 14**
> "For the life of the flesh is in the blood, and I have given it to you on the altar to make atonement for your souls; for it is the blood by reason of the life that makes atonement…
>
> "For as for the life of all flesh, its blood is identified with its life. Therefore I said to the sons of Israel, 'You are not to eat the blood of any flesh, for the life of all flesh is its blood; whoever eats it shall be cut off.'"
>
> **Genesis 9:4**
> "Only you shall not eat flesh with its life, that is, its blood."

God commanded His people not to drink any physical blood because the life of a creature is in its blood. Blood represents life and so the blood of Christ speaks of the actual, real life of Jesus. When we come into covenant with God, we spiritually drink the wine of Jesus' blood and take His life *with all its qualities and power* into our being. As His blood flows into our hearts, it brings His life to every part of our being.

The Exchange

> **John 19:28-30**
> After this, Jesus, knowing that all things had already been accomplished, to fulfil the Scripture, said, "I am thirsty." A jar full of sour wine was standing there; so they put a sponge full of the sour wine upon a branch of hyssop and brought it up to His mouth. Therefore when Jesus had received the sour wine, He said, "It is finished!" And He bowed His head and gave up His spirit.

To fulfil Scripture, Jesus said, "I thirst." Some people then put a sponge full of sour wine on some hyssop and brought it to Christ's mouth.[5] Jesus received the sour wine and then declared, "It is finished!" Having taken the sour wine, His work was complete, and so He gave up His life. But why did

Jesus have to drink the sour wine to complete the work of the cross? What was so important about the sour wine?

The wine of the new covenant is the lifeblood of Christ. It is the energising power of His life, love, purity, and holiness. Just as the sweet wine of the new covenant represents the perfect life of Christ, our old life is also like wine—sour wine. It is ruined by sin and selfishness, and is polluted, corrupt and spiritually sour.

When Jesus drank the sour wine, it was a powerful prophetic act, showing us that Jesus was taking our life of sin into Himself and into death. This is why He could not die until He had received the sour wine. Jesus had to drink in our sinful life to exchange it for His pure life. By taking the sour wine, Jesus was agreeing to exchange our sin for His righteousness, our curse for His blessing, our impurity for His holiness, and our corruption for His perfection.

At the cross Jesus knew what they would bring Him yet still He called out for it. Jesus was thirsty for our sin! He wants it! Even now He cries out, *"Come to me! Give me what I died for! Give me your selfishness, your pride, your greed, your addictions, and your lust. I want it all! Give me your sin, from root to fruit! Surrender the very nature of sin within you so that I can make you truly free! Let me drink in all your sour wine. I'll consume it and I'll give you my wine in return. I'll take your selfishness and give you my selfless love. I'll take your death and give you life. If you are thirsty for righteousness, then come! Let us drink together!"*

Hyssop and Faith

So how do we enter into the reality of this exchange? How do we give our life to Christ and receive His life in return?

> **Exodus 12:21-22**
> Then Moses called for all the elders of Israel and said to them, "Go and take for yourselves lambs according to your families, and slay the Passover lamb. You shall take a bunch of hyssop and dip it in the blood which is in the basin, and apply some of the blood

that is in the basin to the lintel and the two doorposts; and none of you shall go outside the door of his house until morning."

Romans 3:22-25 (NRSV, emphasis added)
For there is no distinction, since all have sinned and fall short of the glory of God; they are now justified by his grace as a gift, through the redemption that is in Christ Jesus, whom God put forward **as a sacrifice of atonement by his blood, effective through faith.**

When they were in Egypt, the people of Israel kept the Passover, which both saved them from death and delivered them from their slavery. This first Passover was a living picture of the cross, where Jesus became our Passover Lamb and sacrificed His life for us.

During the Passover, the Hebrews were not saved simply by the sacrifice of the lamb. Deliverance only came as they acted in faith and applied the blood to their doorposts of their houses with hyssop. Like the people of Israel, we are not delivered from death simply because Jesus died and rose again. Even though the work of the cross is complete and finished, we have to apply His blood to our lives. In this sense, hyssop is a symbol of faith. When we have faith in the blood of Jesus, we can then experience the power of Jesus' blood in our lives.

At the cross, the sour wine was given to Christ on hyssop. This shows us that not only do we receive Christ's life by faith, but we also exchange our broken and sinful life with Jesus by faith. Faith is the key to exchange.

If we lack faith, we need to know that the love of Christ is so intense that He will stop at nothing to bring us into the power of the cross. So if we are struggling to believe in the power of Jesus' blood, then we can ask Him to give us the faith we need to exchange our life for His. If we lack the desire even to truly repent, He is willing to give us a spirit of repentance to help us to come to the cross.[6] Our God of love will always meet us wherever we are and give us whatever we need to take the next step. We simply need to ask.

Summary

Jesus poured out His blood in death that He might give us an inheritance in His life. This inheritance is sealed and secured in His blood. It is ours and nothing can take it away. The awesome indwelling life of Jesus is available to us now by drinking His blood. We simply need to come to Jesus and make a covenant through faith to exchange our life with Him.

As we make this covenant, we find that the blood of Jesus is powerful beyond imagination. Through His blood we are forgiven, redeemed, and no longer subject to God's judgment upon sin. His blood releases us from our bondage to sin and we are set free to live in unity with Jesus. Jesus' blood washes away our sin, making us spiritually clean, innocent, justified and holy. The blood of Christ separates us from the world and devotes us to God.

Jesus' blood contains the fullness of His life. So when we drink His blood by faith, we enter deeper into the reality of being justified, sanctified and cleansed because more of the life of Christ infuses us. We are made righteous because the life of the Righteous One is in us. We are made holy as He is holy because Jesus shares His holiness with us.[7] We are justified because the life of He who did not sin is present in us and we are one with Him. In and of ourselves we have and are nothing, yet as we drink His blood, we enter more into the awesome reality of possessing the life of Jesus within us. For this reason, Jesus says that unless we drink His blood, we can have no life in us.[8] The whole of our relationship with God is made possible through the blood of the cross. And now Jesus calls to us to come, drink, and be one with Him.

Pray

Jesus, I thank you for pouring out your blood for me. Please help me to drink your blood and exchange my life with you. I offer you all my sin, my selfishness, and my corruption. Thank you for washing me clean. Please help me to forget my sin and never bring it back to mind again, ever. Let us live together in your love, purity, and innocence forever.

Study Guide: page 195

6 | Eternal Life

John 6:52-54
The Jews then disputed among themselves, saying, "How can this man give us his flesh to eat?" So Jesus said to them, "Truly, truly, I say to you, unless you eat the flesh of the Son of Man and drink his blood, you have no life in you. Whoever feeds on my flesh and drinks my blood has eternal life, and I will raise him up on the last day."

The blood of Jesus is the basis of our covenant with God and the key to having eternal life. But what really is eternal life?

Eternal Life

John 3:16 (TDB)
"For God so loved the world, that he gave his only Son, that whoever believes in [*eis:* into] him should not perish but have eternal life."

At the cross, God displayed the awesome depths of His love for us. He gave His only Son so that we might not only believe in Jesus but believe into Him. In *First Love,* we saw how the Greek word *eis* means *into* and conveys the sense of a motion into union.[1] Just as a river flows into the sea and becomes one with the ocean, so we are called to believe *into* Jesus and become one with Him. True faith in Christ is so much more than an intellectual belief—it is a powerful movement of the heart into unity with Jesus.

In the same way that unity with Jesus is only found in this present life, so eternal life is a reality that we can experience now through faith. This is made clear in the Greek use of the present tense for the word *have* in this verse. The present tense conveys the sense of an ongoing, habitual or continual action, in the present time. By using the present tense, John makes it clear that eternal life is not simply about a future in heaven. We can experience the gift of eternal life right now as we become one with Jesus.

Knowing God

John 17:1-3

When Jesus had spoken these words, he lifted up his eyes to heaven, and said, "Father, the hour has come; glorify your Son that the Son may glorify you, since you have given him authority over all flesh, to give eternal life to all whom you have given him. And this is eternal life, that they know you, the only true God, and Jesus Christ whom you have sent."

In this passage, Jesus gives eternal life to everyone who is given to Him. And He defines eternal life as knowing God and knowing Jesus whom He sent.

Know: *ginosko* (Greek)
Properly, to know, especially through personal experience. To be taking in knowledge, to come to know, recognise, understand completely.

Know: *yada* (Hebrew)
To know, to be made known or revealed, declare, to cause to know, to know by experience.

The Hebrew word *yada* corresponds to the Greek *ginosko*, which means "to know, especially through personal experience." When used in the context of facts, these words usually speak of having an intellectual understanding. For example, "You know [*ginosko*] that summer is near."[2] However, when used in a relational context, the word *knowledge* takes on a whole new dimension. It no longer speaks of an intellectual knowledge but a relational knowledge that comes through a personal connection.

While we could learn everything there is to know about a person, we could never say that we know that person unless we have a relationship with them. And relationships only come through interaction, communication, and shared experience. It is the same for God. From a relational perspective, learning about God is not the same as knowing God. It is not even close. And yet so many of us are satisfied with just learning about Him. So often we turn

Christianity into a science to be studied rather than a relationship to be enjoyed. Christianity is not like a mathematical problem that can be studied and solved. It is a loving relationship based on two-way interaction. So while it is a great blessing to be able to study the Scriptures and learn about God, we need to remember that the goal of learning is always love—experiential, active, engaged, life-giving, life-changing, life-defining love.[3] With this goal in mind, God is calling us to move from theory into reality. He is calling us to *know* Him.

Intimate Knowledge

Genesis 4:1 (NKJV)
Now Adam knew [*yada*] Eve his wife, and she conceived and bore Cain...

Luke 1:34 (NKJV)
Then Mary said to the angel, "How can this be, since I do not know [*ginosko*] a man?"

There are many different relationships in our natural and spiritual life, each one with a differing kind of knowledge. In this passage, Scripture uses the word *know* to speak of sexual union.[4] Instead of saying "Adam had sexual relations with Eve," Scripture simply says, "Adam knew Eve." This is because making love can be thought of in terms of knowledge—it is the most intimate knowledge we can have of another person. This kind of knowledge is vastly different than the knowledge that is shared between friends, which is different again from the knowledge that a child has of their parents or that a student has of their teacher.

So what kind of knowledge is Jesus speaking about when He says that eternal life is knowing the one true God? When Jesus defines eternal life, He does so entirely within the context of devoted love and unity.[5] Like the knowledge that is shared between a husband and wife, this is a knowledge that is steeped in love, secured in covenant, and expressed in unity.

Covenant

Hosea 2:16, 19-20 (BSB)
"And in that day, declares the LORD, you will call me 'My Husband,' and no longer will you call me 'My Master'…

"So I will betroth you to Me forever; I will betroth you in righteousness and justice, in loving devotion and compassion. And I will betroth you in faithfulness, and you will know the LORD."

In this passage, God makes a covenant with His people so they may *know* Him as their spiritual husband. This intimate knowledge of God is only made possible through the unity that comes from covenant. As we learned earlier, all covenants are designed to create unity. Historically, when people or families entered into a covenant, both parties were prepared to give their lives in order to keep the terms of the covenant. Because it was a matter of life and death, having a covenant with another family would create an unshakeable sense of security and unity in the relationship.

We can see this dynamic at work in marriage. When a man and woman make a marriage covenant, they agree to be exclusively devoted to one another, to love one another, and to create a new life together. This covenant instantly creates a secure environment for unity by protecting each person against the threat of rejection.[6]

In the absence of covenant, there is a risk of very real and lasting damage. When a person gives themselves sexually to someone and is then rejected, it has rippling effects through a person's emotions, psychology, spirituality, and their brain chemistry. In *First Love*, we look at how the brain releases oxytocin in response to love. Oxytocin is known as the "love hormone" or bonding chemical of the brain. It is the warm-fuzzy feeling we get when we are around people who love us. When a couple make love, their brains release oxytocin, which creates a strong sense of emotional unity in the relationship. This then provides a sense of stability for the whole family.

I have a friend who had so many sexual encounters with different people before marriage that now she struggles to feel any emotional unity when she makes love to her husband. Her brain chemistry has changed. I heard it said once that after a rejection, the brain protects itself from further rejection by reducing the level of oxytocin that it releases during sex. The brain continues to respond to each rejection with more self-protection.[7] Once this capacity for emotional unity is lost, it is difficult to rewire the brain and recover the profound sense of unity that God always desired for marriage.

For this reason, Scripture calls us to sexual purity. It is not to take away our fun or deprive us of sexual fulfilment. After all, God *commanded* Adam and Eve to multiply! He wants us to truly enjoy sexual intimacy. He simply knows that in order to experience the real joy and fulfilment of sexual unity, we need to be protected from rejection. And this protection is provided by the covenant of marriage.

Just as it is in the natural realm, deep spiritual intimacy always comes with a sense of vulnerability, even with God. He feels the heartbreak of rejection more deeply than we can imagine. For this reason, Jesus does not share the most intimate affections of His heart with the casual or lukewarm believer. He reserves the depths of His being for those who come into covenant with Him. Until we mature to that point, Jesus meets us where we are and simply calls us deeper. *Come deeper. I want to share more of Myself with you. Come away with Me.*

The depths hold the promise of a greater knowledge of God, but they also require that we give more of ourselves to Him. If we refuse to go deeper, God will maintain the level of intimacy we have allowed Him to have with us. We may still know Him as our saviour, our friend, or as our teacher. God will still speak to us and bless us as much as we allow, but it is not the best for us nor for Him. God is calling us to know Him intimately, and that means we need to make a covenant with Him.

Eternal Love

Luke 10:25-28 (BSB)
One day an expert in the law stood up to test Him. "Teacher," he asked, "what must I do to inherit eternal life?" "What is written in the Law?"

Jesus replied. "How do you read it?" He answered, "'Love the Lord your God with all your heart and with all your soul and with all your strength and with all your mind' and 'Love your neighbour as yourself.'" "You have answered correctly," Jesus said. "Do this and you will live."

In this passage, Jesus sheds even more light on what it means to have eternal life. Eternal life is found in loving God with all our heart, soul, mind and strength, and loving others as if they were us.

Jesus therefore speaks of eternal life both as knowing God and loving Him with all our being. The two always go together. We cannot truly know God without falling in love with Him, and we cannot truly love Him without knowing Him. This means that there is no amount of study or learning that can open the door to knowing Jesus. If our goal is to intimately know God, then we need to start by making a covenant of wholehearted love with Him. If we make the first command our first priority, everything else will follow: knowledge, union, and eternal life.

With this understanding, we could amplify John 3:16 to read:

John 3:16
For God loved the world in this way: He gave His one and only Son, that whoever believes into union with Him shall not perish, but rather know God intimately and love Him with all their heart.

We all know that our life in heaven will be awesome and joyful beyond words. However, we do not need to wait for heaven to experience eternal life. In fact, the love that will flow through us in heaven is exactly the same love that flows through us in this life: it is the love of God! The more that we become channels for His love in this life, the more we can experience eternal life right now.

Life in Christ

> **John 14:6**
> Jesus said to him, "I am the way, and the truth, and the life. No one comes to the Father except through me.
>
> **1 John 5:11 (NASB)**
> And the testimony is this, that God has given us eternal life, and this life is in His Son.

Looking at different passages on eternal life is like turning a diamond and seeing a different colour. The light and the diamond remain the same, but the expression changes in glory. There is a glory in seeing eternal life as intimate knowledge or as wholehearted love or as a spiritual union. But these are all simply colours of the Light of Christ. God has given us eternal life and this life is in His Son. Eternal life is not something that God has and then gives to us. Jesus Christ Himself is eternal life.

We can think of this like we think of love. God does not give us His love as a gift that is separate from Himself. When God gives us the gift of love, He gives it to us by giving us Himself. He loved us when He gave Jesus at the cross. He continues to love us by filling us over and over with His Spirit of love. Through His indwelling Spirit, the love of God becomes our possession and possessor. He is the gift.

In the same way, Jesus is the gift of eternal life. When we believe into Jesus and we drink His blood through faith, we have eternal life because Jesus is life and we both possess Him and are possessed by Him. Through our unity with Jesus, we can experience and enjoy all the glorious colours of eternal life.

> **1 John 5:20**
> And we know that the Son of God has come and has given us understanding, so that we may know him who is true; and we are in him who is true, in his Son Jesus Christ. He is the true God and eternal life.

God has given us understanding that we may *know* Him who is true. And we are *in* Him. And He *is* eternal life. This verse provides a beautiful summary of the amazing gospel of love, bringing together knowing God, living in unity with Jesus, and possessing eternal life. So in summary:

- We experience eternal life by knowing God
- We can only know God through wholehearted, interactive love
- The first command of love is our marriage covenant with Jesus
- As we make this covenant with Jesus, we become His bride
- In marriage, we are our Beloved's and He is ours. Our life is now one of mutual possession
- Our covenant allows us to experience increasingly greater depths of life through love, intimacy, and unity with Jesus
- This is all possible because Jesus is eternal life and He lives within us

Our faith begins, continues, and ends in a union with Jesus. Time is short, so let us cast aside every distraction and focus on making a covenant of love so that we might truly know God. This is where eternal life is found, and it is a life that lasts forever!

Pray

Father! I love you and I want to love you more! I want to know you more! I repent for my lack of devotion, for tolerating distractions and letting my affections wander. I choose wholehearted love. I give you my entire heart, and those areas of my heart that I cannot give, I ask you to take. Let us be one, now and forever!

7 | Stages of Covenant

Genesis 17:1-11 (NKJV)

When Abram was ninety-nine years old, the Lord appeared to Abram and said to him, "I am Almighty God; walk before Me and be blameless. And I will make My covenant between Me and you, and will multiply you exceedingly." Then Abram fell on his face, and God talked with him, saying: "As for Me, behold, My covenant is with you, and you shall be a father of many nations. No longer shall your name be called Abram, but your name shall be Abraham; for I have made you a father of many nations. I will make you exceedingly fruitful; and I will make nations of you, and kings shall come from you. And I will establish My covenant between Me and you and your descendants after you in their generations, for an everlasting covenant, to be God to you and your descendants after you. Also I give to you and your descendants after you the land in which you are a stranger, all the land of Canaan, as an everlasting possession; and I will be their God."

And God said to Abraham: "As for you, you shall keep My covenant, you and your descendants after you throughout their generations. This is My covenant which you shall keep, between Me and you and your descendants after you: Every male child among you shall be circumcised; and you shall be circumcised in the flesh of your foreskins, and it shall be a sign of the covenant between Me and you."

In this passage, God gives Abram a new name: Abraham. He then calls Abraham to circumcise his flesh as a sign of the covenant. Long after he was originally called, Abraham is required to pay a personal price to be in covenant with God. This cut in the flesh was more than a simple act of obedience—it was a powerful prophetic act representing the spiritual reality at the foundation of covenant. This single act connects God's covenant with Abraham to the Mosaic covenant, and on to its ultimate fulfilment in the covenant of Jesus Christ.

Covenant Continued
Exodus 6:2-9

God spoke to Moses and said to him, "I am the LORD. I appeared to Abraham, to Isaac, and to Jacob, as God Almighty, but by my name the LORD I did not make myself known to them. I also established my covenant with them to give them the land of Canaan, the land in which they lived as sojourners. Moreover, I have heard the groaning of the people of Israel whom the Egyptians hold as slaves, and I have remembered my covenant. Say therefore to the people of Israel, 'I am the LORD, and I will bring you out from under the burdens of the Egyptians, and I will deliver you from slavery to them, and I will redeem you with an outstretched arm and with great acts of judgment. I will take you to be my people, and I will be your God, and you shall know that I am the LORD your God, who has brought you out from under the burdens of the Egyptians. I will bring you into the land that I swore to give to Abraham, to Isaac, and to Jacob. I will give it to you for a possession. I am the LORD.'" Moses spoke thus to the people of Israel, but they did not listen to Moses, because of their broken spirit and harsh slavery.

God was bound to the people of Israel because of His covenant with Abraham. In this passage, God remembers His covenant to Abraham and so promises the people of Israel to be their God, to take them as His people, and to bring them into a land of their own.

In many ways, the journeys of Abraham and the people of Israel are like living parables for our journey in Christ. As He does for one, God does for many. Abraham was called to leave Assyria; Israel was called to leave Egypt. Abraham was brought into a blood-covenant with God through the passing between the pieces of the sacrifices; Israel was brought into a blood-covenant through the keeping of the Passover and the sprinkling of the blood in the wilderness. Abraham was circumcised in Canaan; Israel was circumcised at Gilgal.

In both journeys, we see a staged process to covenant. Each stage ensured a greater level of blessing and abundance, but also required a greater level of obedience and sacrificial response to God.

In the first stage of covenant, the people of Israel simply had to apply the blood of the Passover lamb to their homes and allow God to set them free. In His grace, God demanded nothing from His people except that they follow Him out of Egypt. They did, and they were free.

Once Israel had crossed the Red Sea and entered safely into the Sinai, God then gave Moses the *Torah* and showed His people what it meant to live in covenant with Him. He then invited them to embrace a greater level of love and devotion.

> **Deuteronomy 6:1-5** (NASB, emphasis added)
> "Now this is **the commandment**, and these are the statutes and judgments which the LORD your God has commanded to teach you, that you may observe them in the land which you are crossing over to possess, that you may fear the LORD your God, to keep all His statutes and His commandments which I command you, you and your son and your grandson, all the days of your life, and that your days may be prolonged. Therefore hear, O Israel, and **be careful to observe it**, that it may be well with you, and that you may multiply greatly as the LORD God of your fathers has promised you—'a land flowing with milk and honey.'
>
> "Hear, O Israel: The LORD our God, the LORD is one! You shall love the LORD your God with all your heart, with all your soul, and with all your strength."

The *Torah* literally means *Instruction* or *Direction* and it is the name given to the first five books of the Bible. The Torah contains many statutes and judgments, but they are all based on **the one commandment**: to love God with all the heart, mind, soul and strength. All the other rules and statutes in the Mosaic writings are simply outworkings of this one command.[1]

In *First Love,* we look at the metaphor of the clockmaker. If we made a clock and we had to give it just one command, we would simply say, *Tell the time*. Within that command we would communicate the whole design and purpose of our creation. This is what God does in this passage. By giving us one command, God reveals that He has perfectly designed us for love.

Many people overlook the Old Testament, failing to see its relevance to our faith in Christ. Yet this command is not simply relevant to our faith, it is paramount. Jesus Himself confirms the place of the first command. It will always be God's highest priority because it will always be the primary revelation of God's unchanging design for us. Even into eternity, there will be only one design and one command: to love God with our entire being.

Circumcision and Covenant

Once we made our clock, it would depend on us for the energy it needs to function. Therefore, if we made a covenant with our clock, we would say, *"I'll give you everything you need. I'll keep all your mechanics working and I'll refresh your batteries. All you need to do is keep telling the time."*

In the same way, the command of wholehearted love is not only a statement of design—it is the basis of our covenant relationship with God. But like a clock that cannot power itself, we cannot generate our own love. We need God to make it possible. But can we trust God to empower us to love Him with our entire being?

> **Deuteronomy 30:6** (NASB)
> "Moreover the Lord your God will circumcise your heart and the heart of your descendants, to love the Lord your God with all your heart and with all your soul, so that you may live."

Here we see God's unbreakable promise of power. If we choose to love Him with all our heart and soul, He will make it possible. How will He do it? Through the circumcision of the heart. This is why God called Abraham to participate in the covenant through circumcision saying:

Genesis 17:10-11 (NASB)

"This is My covenant, which you shall keep, between Me and you and your descendants after you: every male among you shall be circumcised. And you shall be circumcised in the flesh of your foreskin; and it shall be the sign of the covenant between Me and you."

The circumcision of the flesh was an outward sign of God's covenant of love. In this respect, circumcision was given to the Jews as a *type*—a physical symbol of a spiritual reality.[2] When Israel circumcised their children, they performed a prophetic act that spoke of a reality that would ultimately be fulfilled in Christ.

Romans 2:28-29
For no one is a Jew who is merely one outwardly, nor is circumcision outward and physical. But a Jew is one inwardly, and circumcision is a matter of the heart, by the Spirit, not by the letter. His praise is not from man but from God.

In itself, physical circumcision of the flesh is of no spiritual benefit at all. Because the type is fulfilled in Christ, Scripture makes it clear that we do not need to be physically circumcised—it is the circumcision of the heart alone that matters.[3] It has always been this way. Moses called the people of Israel to circumcise their hearts; Jeremiah warned of God's judgment upon those who were not circumcised in their heart; Ezekiel banned anyone with an uncircumcised heart from entering the sanctuary; Stephen rebuked the Pharisees for being uncircumcised in heart; Paul declared that true Jews are circumcised in heart, and Jesus said that holiness is all about the heart.[4]

There is only one way to keep the greatest command. We must let Jesus circumcise our hearts so that we might love Him with all our heart and soul. If we are willing, He is able.

Pray

Father, thank you for designing me for love. Thank you for promising to make it possible for me to love you with all my heart. Please take me on this journey.

PART TWO | SPIRIT AND FLESH

8 | The Flesh

> Galatians 5:16-21
> But I say, walk by the Spirit, and you will not gratify the desires of the flesh. For the desires of the flesh are against the Spirit, and the desires of the Spirit are against the flesh, for these are opposed to each other, to keep you from doing the things you want to do. But if you are led by the Spirit, you are not under the law. Now the works of the flesh are evident: sexual immorality, impurity, sensuality, idolatry, sorcery, enmity, strife, jealousy, fits of anger, rivalries, dissensions, divisions, envy, drunkenness, orgies, and things like these. I warn you, as I warned you before, that those who do such things will not inherit the kingdom of God.

Before we look at the circumcision of the heart, we need to look at what Scripture calls *the flesh*. Scripture uses this word in a variety of different ways. In a physical context, it can refer to the meat of animals, a person's body, or physical life itself. In a spiritual context, as in the passage above, the word *flesh* is used to refer to the corrupting force of sin within us.[1]

The flesh primarily expresses itself through an instinct to sin. Because the flesh motivates us on an instinctive rather than a logical level, it can be rightly thought of as a *nature*—an inner force that compels our natural or subconscious behaviour. For this reason, some Bible translations use the terms *sinful nature* or *selfish desires* when translating the word *flesh*.[2] For the purposes of this book, we will use the terms sinful nature, selfish nature, flesh nature, and old self interchangeably to refer to the flesh.

The driving force of the flesh nature is pure selfishness. This selfishness forms sinful instincts which then shape our thinking and corrupt our sense of identity and purpose. The flesh constantly compels us to pursue pleasure, self-gratification, self-reliance, and material security. Instead of affirming our design of love, the flesh imposes its own design of selfishness upon us. In every way, the flesh is the archenemy of love.

Flesh and the Body

> **Mark 7:20-23**
> And he [Jesus] said, "What comes out of a person is what defiles him. For from within, out of the heart of man, come evil thoughts, sexual immorality, theft, murder, adultery, coveting, wickedness, deceit, sensuality, envy, slander, pride, foolishness. All these evil things come from within, and they defile a person."

When reading Scriptures that use the word *flesh* in a spiritual way, we need to be careful not to confuse it with the physical body. While sin affects our body, the body is not the source of sin. For as Jesus says: all our evil thoughts and desires flow from our spiritual heart rather than our physical body.

> **Galatians 5:24**
> And those who belong to Christ Jesus have crucified the flesh with its passions and desires.

By calling us to crucify the flesh, Scripture again separates the flesh nature from our physical body. For God does not want us to physically crucify our bodies in order to find freedom from our evil instincts and desires. Rather, Scripture calls us to spiritually experience the power of the cross to crucify our flesh nature.

The Origin of the Flesh

> **Matthew 13:24-30**
> He put another parable before them, saying, "The kingdom of heaven may be compared to a man who sowed good seed in his field, but while his men were sleeping, his enemy came and sowed weeds among the wheat and went away. So when the plants came up and bore grain,

then the weeds appeared also. And the servants of the master of the house came and said to him, 'Master, did you not sow good seed in your field? How then does it have weeds?' He said to them, 'An enemy has done this.' So the servants said to him, 'Then do you want us to go and gather them?' But he said, 'No, lest in gathering the weeds you root up the wheat along with them. Let both grow together until the harvest, and at harvest time I will tell the reapers, "Gather the weeds first and bind them in bundles to be burned, but gather the wheat into my barn."'"

Humanity is God's field. God created us to be sown with His seed and fruitful in His love. But an enemy came and sowed his seed in God's field.

This enemy came to humanity in the Garden of Eden in the form of a serpent. In a moment of time, the serpent deceived Adam and Eve into making a series of choices. Adam and Eve acted on Satan's lie and in doing so they chose rebellion over obedience. Instead of talking to God about the temptation, they chose to act independently and end their dependence on God. By using their own strength to take a blessing for themselves, they chose legalism over grace. By eating the fruit, they chose to disconnect their hearts from God's and unite themselves with a different nature: *the flesh*.

The fall of humanity was the enemy's greatest and most devastating work. Through one deception, Satan successfully implanted his nature into the hearts of God's creation, cursing us with a basic instinct of selfishness, pride, lust, insecurity, greed and independence. Ever since the Fall, the seed of our enemy has been passed down from one generation to the next.

> **1 John 3:8**
> Whoever makes a practice of sinning is of the devil, for the devil has been sinning from the beginning. The reason the Son of God appeared was to destroy the works of the devil.

No one can ever free themselves from their own selfish nature. We all need a saviour. Thank God that Jesus appeared to destroy the works of Satan! His whole goal in coming to earth was to destroy the work of Satan by breaking the curse of the sinful nature.

Hostility

Romans 8:1-8

There is therefore now no condemnation for those who are in Christ Jesus. For the law of the Spirit of life has set you free in Christ Jesus from the law of sin and death. For God has done what the law, weakened by the flesh, could not do. By sending his own Son in the likeness of sinful flesh and for sin, he condemned sin in the flesh, in order that the righteous requirement of the law might be fulfilled in us, who walk not according to the flesh but according to the Spirit. For those who live according to the flesh set their minds on the things of the flesh, but those who live according to the Spirit set their minds on the things of the Spirit. For to set the mind on the flesh is death, but to set the mind on the Spirit is life and peace. For the mind that is set on the flesh is hostile to God, for it does not submit to God's law; indeed, it cannot. Those who are in the flesh cannot please God.

To live according to the flesh is to have our mindsets and thoughts shaped by our sinful nature. As this passage shows, the flesh is hostile towards God and opposed to His Spirit of love in every way possible.

- The Spirit of God gives us life; the flesh brings death
- The Spirit guides us into truth; the flesh deceives us with lies
- The Spirit leads us into reality; the flesh delights in fantasy
- The Spirit calls us into joy; the flesh craves entertainment
- The Spirit empowers and edifies us; the flesh sabotages our lives
- The Spirit leads us to selflessly love; the flesh leads us to act selfishly
- The Spirit restores our spiritual value; the flesh makes us act without love and so reduces us to nothing[3]
- The Spirit inspires us to give; the flesh motivates us to take
- The Spirit compels us to love; the flesh dominates us with lust[4]

- The Spirit leads us to connect in meaningful relationships; the flesh leads us to isolate ourselves
- The Spirit returns us to a place of significance; the flesh robs us of all significance
- The Spirit restores our design of love; the flesh corrupts our design with selfishness and sin

The gospel of Christ is as opposed to the flesh nature as it is to the forces of Satan. Like Satan, the selfish nature always seeks to kill, steal and destroy. It kills our time, steals our calling, and destroys our design. Every time we act according to the flesh it brings spiritual death and robs the world of the life that is released when we love.[5] The cost is heart-breaking.

Both Spirit and flesh battle to possess our hearts and rule over our souls, and neither wants to share. But the good news is that this battle does not have to go on forever. God has condemned the flesh. He has passed judgment on our selfish nature and sentenced it to death.

The Law and the Flesh

Romans 7:5-12

For while we were living in the flesh, our sinful passions, aroused by the law, were at work in our members to bear fruit for death. But now we are released from the law, having died to that which held us captive, so that we serve in the new way of the Spirit and not in the old way of the written code.

What then shall we say? That the law is sin? By no means! Yet if it had not been for the law, I would not have known sin. For I would not have known what it is to covet if the law had not said, "You shall not covet." But sin, seizing an opportunity through the commandment, produced in me all kinds of covetousness. For apart from the law, sin lies dead. I was once alive apart from the law, but when the commandment came, sin came alive and I died. The very commandment that promised life proved to be death to me. For sin, seizing an opportunity through the commandment, deceived me and through it killed me. So the law is holy, and the commandment is holy and righteous and good.

In this passage, Paul describes the relationship between the law and the flesh. The law is important because unless a command is given, there can be no opportunity for obedience nor rebellion. For example, if young children are playing near a bowl of fruit, they will generally not take the fruit unless they are hungry. But that changes when we give them a command about the fruit. *Now children, do not eat the fruit in this bowl!* As soon as the command is given, a desire is often aroused, even in those who are not actually hungry. Why does the desire only appear when the command is given? Because it is not created by hunger but by the instinctive nature of the flesh to rebel. This usually produces conflict within the heart. *I know I'm not supposed to eat the fruit, but I really want it. That apple looks so good...*

The goal of the law was never to control our behaviour. It was never about making us strive in our own strength to overcome sin. The commands of the law were given to expose the selfishness within our hearts and lead us by faith to the cross. We can think of the law like a medical scan that identifies the cancer in our hearts so we can take the next step: heart transplant surgery. The fact that the law exposes the cancer of selfishness does not make the law evil. In fact, it makes the law holy and righteous and good. The law works for our good by diagnosing our problem and pointing us to the solution before it is too late.

We should not be afraid to let the commands of Scripture spiritually diagnose us. The Holy Spirit can use the commands within the word of God to show us areas where we need to change and grow. The key is to let the commands of Scripture lead us into a greater degree of faith and unity with Jesus rather than a greater level of striving and effort. In order to do this, we need to overcome legalism.

In many religious circles, the work of the law is completely disconnected from faith. Sermon after sermon, the commands of Scripture are preached through a lens of legalism rather than love. These commands identify the problem but so often we are not led to the Solution. The message of legalism constantly tells us that we are not good enough and we have to try harder to behave righteously. This is like receiving a medical scan that shows us we have cancer, then hearing the doctor say, "You need to try harder to be well." Instead of seeking life-saving surgery, we try to fix the symptoms without going to the root cause. We think, *I will try harder to eat well, sleep well, and exercise well. Maybe next time the scan will be different.* This makes no sense in the physical realm and even less sense spiritually. Just as a medical scan cannot cure cancer, so the commands of Scripture "are of no value in stopping the indulgence of the flesh."[6] Our greatest striving is vanity, and our best efforts are all worthless.

Because the flesh nature operates on an instinctive level, we cannot overcome it through our works, and neither can we teach our way out of the flesh. This is why decades of sermons often produce so little change in people. No logical argument or religious philosophy can ever deliver us from our addictive selfishness. Of all the world's religions, only Christianity truly recognises the selfish nature that ravages the heart of humanity, and Scripture alone reveals the one true solution: the cross.

Pray

Father, I know I am far from perfect. You know I was born selfish and grew up outside your design of love. Thank you for taking my sin. I want to be truly pure and holy before you. Please show me the power of Jesus' blood to overcome my flesh nature. I know you can do it.

9 | Identity

Before we look at the cross, we need to understand what the selfish nature is and how it impacts our identity.

> **Ephesians 4:20-24** (NASB)
> But that is not the way you learned Christ!— assuming that you have heard about him and were taught in him, as the truth is in Jesus, to put off your old self, which belongs to your former manner of life and is corrupt through deceitful desires, and to be renewed in the spirit of your minds, and to put on the new self, created after the likeness of God in true righteousness and holiness.

> **Colossians 3:5-10**
> Put to death therefore what is earthly in you: sexual immorality, impurity, passion, evil desire, and covetousness, which is idolatry. On account of these the wrath of God is coming. In these you too once walked, when you were living in them. But now you must put them all away: anger, wrath, malice, slander, and obscene talk from your mouth. Do not lie to one another, seeing that you have put off the old self with its practices and have put on the new self, which is being renewed in knowledge after the image of its creator.

In this passage, the *flesh* is referred to as the *old self*. The sense here is that the flesh is connected to our sense of self-perception and identity. Because we grow up with a selfish nature, it is natural for us to identify ourselves with the different instincts of the flesh—lust, pride, greed, anger and so on. We see the dark side of our heart and believe that it is a part of us. Our focus then shifts to managing and suppressing the darkness. We seek counselling and read self-improvement books that call us to embrace our brokenness and love ourselves the way we are. So we try to love ourselves in spite of the darkness we see and feel within. But it never works. Why? Because the old self is utterly unlovable. It is not a broken bone that needs healing but a deadly cancer that needs destroying. The flesh nature is an irredeemable evil, worthy only of death.

> **Romans 7:16-20**
> Now if I do what I do not want, I agree with the law, that it is good. So now it is no longer I who do it, but sin that dwells within me. For I know that nothing good dwells in me, that is, in my flesh. For I have the desire to do what is right, but not the ability to carry it out. For I do not do the good I want, but the evil I do not want is what I keep on doing. Now if I do what I do not want, it is no longer I who do it, but sin that dwells within me.

Here Paul speaks of the old self or flesh nature simply as *sin that dwells within me*. He repeats himself deliberately to make a point concerning identity. *If I do what I do not want, it is **no longer I** who do it, but sin that dwells within me.* Paul deliberately separates his own identity from the selfish nature. He knows it is not him. Like Paul, when we act selfishly against our own will, it is not we who do the action. Rather, the motivating force behind the action is the selfish nature. It is not us.

Passing the blame for sin onto our selfish nature in no way excuses us from the consequences of our actions. On the contrary, we are accountable for everything that we allow the old self to do through us. However, in terms of our identity, Scripture makes it clear: we are not our flesh. The flesh nature is greedy, lustful, proud, vengeful, insecure, unforgiving, boastful, spiteful, deceitful, divisive, selfish and mean. And though it may temporarily live within us, it is not us. Our call is to lay aside the old self and put on our new self. This is our true identity which God has created in His image and likeness. It is loving, kind, generous, compassionate, zealous, peaceful, forgiving, humble, secure and selfless. This is who we truly are in Christ.

Separating Holy from Unholy
Ezekiel 44:23 (NKJV)
And they shall teach My people the difference between the holy and the unholy, and cause them to discern between the unclean and the clean.

God calls all His people to separate the holy from the unholy, the precious from the worthless. So how do we separate holy from unholy? In Christ, holiness is an inward reality. Within us, we have a holy spirit nature and an unholy selfish nature. Our call is not merely to physically separate ourselves from unholy things, but to separate ourselves spiritually from our old self. This means that we need to learn to discern the difference between our spirit and flesh and begin to see ourselves for who we truly are in union with Jesus: a new creation, made in the image and likeness of Love.

For many of us, this can be incredibly difficult. The selfish nature has had years to shape our thoughts and feelings, including our basic instincts. So often our first reaction to a situation is not one of selfless love but one of selfishness—*how can I protect or serve myself in this situation?* Because the flesh influences us at such a subconscious level, it naturally becomes the dominant force in our identity. We think that because we have always lived with a measure of anxiety that it is a part of who we are—a weakness in our personality. The same is true for all the fruit of the flesh. Because we have grown up experiencing ongoing lust or pride or greed, we believe that our personality is inherently flawed. This perception then creates space for self-hatred. We see the different aspects of our selfish nature and are repulsed by them. But what we fail to understand is that everything we want to hate about ourselves is not actually us. It is the flesh, and it did not come from God. The enemy planted the weeds of sin in our heart and they must be removed.

If only our suicidal youth understood their design of love. If only they knew that everything they hate in themselves is not truly them. If only we could all separate the flesh from the spirit in ourselves and each other. Imagine the freedom.

I was once praying for a woman and in my heart, I saw a picture of a blade of wheat. Around the wheat was a weed, twisted so tightly that the wheat and the weed looked almost one. God was giving me an insight into the woman's sense of identity. There was no separation between her selfish nature and her spirit nature, so she was believing that she was a mixture of good and evil. When I shared this with her, the tears flowed, and I could sense the struggle. *Could I dare to believe that I am truly and only good in Christ? After everything I've been told, after a lifetime of sin-shaped thought about myself, could I dare to believe that my flesh is not me?*

I once heard a man share a similar vision. In the vision, he saw a beautiful woman dressed like a bride. She was lying on her back, half asleep with her eyes closed. On her face was a large and very deadly spider. Time after time, the spider would lower its body close to her face and sink its fangs into her, filling her with poison. Because of her slumber, the woman was unaware of what was happening. In fact, she was stroking the spider's back as it gently killed her. God showed the man that the spider was the flesh nature. It was a deadly evil that the people of God were embracing.

The message of the vision is clear: we need to wake up and open our eyes. When we see the selfish nature for what it is, our true instincts will take over. Like a person who wakes up to find a spider on their face, we will move to separate what is holy (us) from what is unholy (the selfish nature). And we will do it quickly.

New Flesh

John 6:51-58

"I am the living bread that came down out of heaven; if anyone eats of this bread, he will live forever; and the bread also which I will give for the life of the world is My flesh." Then the Jews began to argue with one another, saying, "How can this man give us His flesh to eat?" So Jesus said to them, "Truly, truly, I say to you, unless you eat the flesh of the Son of Man and drink His blood, you have no life in yourselves. He who eats My flesh and drinks My blood has eternal life, and I will raise him up on the last day. For My flesh is true food, and My blood is true drink. He who eats My flesh and drinks My blood abides in Me, and I in him. As the living Father sent Me, and I live because of the Father, so he who eats Me, he also will live because of Me. This is the bread which came down out of heaven; not as the fathers ate and died; he who eats this bread will live forever."

The bread that Jesus gives for the life of the world is His flesh. If we want to live, then we need to learn what it means to eat the flesh of Christ. This call has no physical aspect to it. Just as we cannot drink Christ's physical blood, so we cannot eat His physical body. God is spirit and so we are called to eat the *spiritual* flesh of Christ.[1] But what is the flesh of Christ?

In the last chapter, we saw how Scripture uses the word *flesh* as a metaphor for the sinful and corrupt nature within people. Yet Jesus' flesh—His nature—is not corrupt in any way. His divine nature is sinless and perfect. Like the Passover lamb, Jesus was a sacrificial offering that was without any blemish. Like the unleavened bread, His flesh was without the yeast of sin and corruption. So when Scripture speaks of the flesh of Christ, it is speaking of His perfect, pure, righteous, holy and uncorrupted nature.

> **2 Peter 1:3-4**
> His divine power has granted to us all things that pertain to life and godliness, through the knowledge of him who called us to his own glory and excellence, by which he has granted to us his precious and very great promises, so that through them you may become partakers of the divine nature, having escaped from the corruption that is in the world because of sinful desire.

To eat the flesh of Christ is to partake of the divine nature of Jesus. This is the key to transformation. Our call is not to learn to live like Jesus, but to take hold of His magnificent promises and partake of His nature. Only then will we discover our true identity in union with Jesus.

So what is the nature of Jesus like?

1 John 4:16
We have come to know and have believed the love which God has for us. God is love, and the one who abides in love abides in God, and God abides in him.

Hebrews 12:28-29
Therefore, since we receive a kingdom which cannot be shaken, let us show gratitude, by which we may offer to God an acceptable service with reverence and awe; for our God is a consuming fire.

Galatians 5:22-23
But the fruit of the Spirit is love, joy, peace, patience, kindness, goodness, faithfulness, gentleness, self-control; against such things there is no law.

The nature of Jesus is revealed in Scripture. He is God, and He is love. He is not a quiet or timid love, but an awesome consuming fire of love. All the different qualities of His character—His holiness, power, grace, joy, zeal, goodness, peace, wisdom and so on—they are all found in His nature of pure love.

What we consume becomes a part of us. It is therefore important that we have a vision not just to experience different aspects of the nature of God, but to become one with His nature. For example, when God reveals the majesty of His goodness to us, we need to receive that goodness into the very core of our being and let it become our part of us. This is what it means to partake of the nature of Christ. The more we consume His love, the more His love consumes us!

Compelled by Love

2 Corinthians 5:14
For the love of Christ compels us, because we judge thus: that if one died for all, then all died.

When we eat of Christ, our heart of stone is replaced with a heart of His flesh and our very nature is changed.[2] Our nature is the spiritual force within us that shapes our instincts, our character, our thoughts, our motives and our actions. The more we partake of Jesus' nature, the more His love shapes our character. Then, instead of our sinful nature compelling us to sin, His nature within us will compel us to think, speak and act in love.

Pray

Lord, I am sorry for tolerating the selfish nature in my life. I am sorry for letting it shape my identity. I know it was never a part of my design. Please help me to truly separate my true self from my old self. Help me to see myself through your eyes.

10 | Circumcising the Heart

Matthew 26:26-28
Now as they were eating, Jesus took bread, and after blessing it broke it and gave it to the disciples, and said, "Take, eat; this is my body." And he took a cup, and when he had given thanks he gave it to them, saying, "Drink of it, all of you, for this is my blood of the covenant, which is poured out for many for the forgiveness of sins."

Forgiveness is a priceless gift bought by the blood of Christ. But why did Jesus have to shed His blood in order to forgive our sin?

Remember God's covenant with Abraham. The Son passed between the pieces and made a blood covenant with the Father on Abraham's behalf. The blood was an essential part of this covenant because it represented the new life that was created through covenant. Our covenant with God is the same. It is not simply a case of receiving forgiveness from Jesus or making an agreement with Him. It is about coming into union with Jesus and sharing His life.

All through Scripture, life is defined in terms of love. *We know that we have passed out of death into life, because we love. Whoever does not love abides in death.*[1] *God will empower us to love Him with all our heart and soul, so that we may live.*[2] *How do we inherit eternal life? Love forever!*[3] Life and love are inseparably connected. When we agree to a covenant-life with Jesus, we agree to share a life of selfless love with Him. However, the opposite is also true. Apart from Christ, all of us have sinned and fallen short of the glory of God's design of love. Like all people throughout history, we inherited a sinful nature and when we first acted according to our sin nature, we chose selfishness over love. This immediately brought us into a covenant with death.

Because of our agreement with death, Satan stands like a prosecutor in court, claiming us for himself and demanding the death penalty for our sin. Thankfully, when Jesus made covenant with the Father on our behalf, He took on the responsibility for our failure. From the very beginning, Jesus knew that He would die for our sins, and He was willing to die because He also knew our value. Restoring our design as channels of the Father's love was worth the greatest sacrifice in all eternity.

The life and death nature of covenant is why Jesus had to give His blood in order to restore us into covenant with God. The blood of Christ paid for our violation of covenant and secured the forgiveness of our debt. His blood also cancelled our covenant with death and selfishness and replaced it with a new covenant of life based on union with God. With our debt paid and a new covenant in place, Satan lost the legal authority to demand our death or condemnation.

The gift of forgiveness is an awesome blessing, however it does not restore our design of love. It simply deals with the fruit of our selfish nature by cleansing our guilt and forgiving the debt we incur with every loveless action we do. If we want to be truly free, we need to look to the cross and see beyond forgiveness.

Taking Away Sin

When Jesus came, John the Baptist prophesied that the axe was coming to the root of the tree.[4] Instead of merely dealing with the fruit of our sinful acts through forgiveness, Jesus was going to deal with the root: our sinful nature.

> **Matthew 1:21**
> "She will bear a son, and you shall call his name Jesus, for he will save his people from their sins."

> **John 1:29**
> The next day he saw Jesus coming toward him, and said, "Behold, the Lamb of God, who takes away the sin of the world!"

Jesus came as the Lamb of God to take away the sin of the world. The Greek word translated as *take away,* means essentially the same as in English. The idea is that something is taken and removed away from its original place. So where is the original place of sin? It is only within the hearts of people. And what does it mean for Jesus to take away sin? It can only mean one thing: Through the cross, Jesus removes the full root of sin and selfishness from our hearts and takes it into death itself. And it is finished.

> **Colossians 3:9-10** (NASB)
> Do not lie to one another, since you laid aside [*apekdyomai*] the old self with its evil practices, and have put on the new self who is being renewed to a true knowledge according to the image of the One who created him…
>
> **Lay aside:** *apekdyomai*
> Wholly put off from one's self (denoting separation from what is put off); wholly to strip off for one's self (for one's own advantage).

In Christ, we are a new creation, created in the image of God.[5] However, we cannot truly become this new creation until we put off our old self. To lay aside the old self means that we are to *wholly* separate ourselves from our flesh nature. Nothing in these verses calls us to manage, deny, or hide our selfish nature. Rather, we are called to entirely strip ourselves of the flesh. All sin must go.

Many of us have grown so used to the presence of the selfish nature in our lives that it can be challenging to imagine wholly separating ourselves from it. Every time we sense it rising up within us, we slowly back away from our sin, like a person retreating from a poisonous snake. We poke sticks at the snake and try to keep it at bay, making it our goal not to get bitten again. Yet God has a completely different goal for us. He is calling us to turn our back on the snake of sin and run full speed into His design of love. If we would choose to pursue this life of love, God guarantees to do what we could never do by ourselves: He will crush the head of the snake Himself.

Circumcised in the Removal

Colossians 2:9-12 (NASB)
For in Him all the fullness of Deity dwells in bodily form, and in Him you have been made complete, and He is the head over all rule and authority; and in Him you were also circumcised with a circumcision made without hands, in the removal [*apekdyomai*] of the body of the flesh by the circumcision of Christ; having been buried with Him in baptism, in which you were also raised up with Him through faith in the working of God, who raised Him from the dead.

Colossians 2:11 (NLT)
... you were "circumcised," but not by a physical procedure. Christ performed a spiritual circumcision--the cutting away of your sinful nature.

In the natural realm, physical circumcision is made by the severing and removal of the foreskin. When God gave Abraham the sign of circumcision, it was a prophetic act that represented a far superior spiritual circumcision. The circumcision of the heart would not involve just the removal of a small part of the flesh, but the total removal of the entire sinful nature. Scripture is clear and so there can be no room for doubt: In Christ we are circumcised with a spiritual circumcision by the removal of the entirety (*body*) of the sinful nature (*flesh*). This is made possible by the circumcision of Christ—His death on the cross.

John 8:31-36
So Jesus said to the Jews who had believed him, "If you abide in my word, you are truly my disciples, and you will know the truth, and the truth will set you free." They answered him, "We are offspring of Abraham and have never been enslaved to anyone. How is it that you say, 'You will become free'?"

Jesus answered them, "Truly, truly, I say to you, everyone who practices sin is a slave to sin. The slave does not remain in the house forever; the son remains forever. So if the Son sets you free, you will be free indeed."

Galatians 5:24
And those who belong to Christ Jesus have crucified the flesh with its passions and desires.

The flesh nature rules over people through its instinct to sin and so everyone who practices sin is a slave to their sinful nature. Yet total freedom from indwelling sin can be found in Jesus.

When we are ready to be crucified with Christ, Jesus takes us into death with Him. He cuts away our selfish nature and removes the source of all our sinful instincts—*all of them*. This brings transformation at the deepest, most instinctive level. Jesus takes every sinful passion, every perverse desire, and every selfish motive, and He exchanges them with His nature of love. Christ's love then becomes our primary instinct. This is the awesome power of the cross and it is how Jesus makes us free indeed.

Deuteronomy 30:6, 11 (NASB)
"Moreover the Lord your God will circumcise your heart and the heart of your descendants, to love the Lord your God with all your heart and with all your soul, so that you may live....

"For this commandment which I command you today is not too difficult for you, nor is it out of reach."

The Father knows that there is no way we can keep the greatest command of wholehearted love while our hearts are divided. We cannot be both selfless *and* selfish. Nor can we love God with *all* our heart while the selfish nature possesses *any* part of our heart. Therefore God promises to remove the selfish nature from our hearts so that we can love Him with all our heart and soul. It is not too difficult for Him, so it is not out of reach for us.

1 Thessalonians 5:23-24 (emphasis added)
Now may the God of peace himself sanctify you completely, and may your whole spirit and soul and body be kept blameless at the coming of our Lord Jesus Christ. He who calls you is faithful; **he will surely do it.**

Again we see that what is impossible for people is possible for God. He can sanctify us *completely*. And if we are willing, He will surely do it.

It is important that we understand why we can fully trust God's promise of a circumcised heart. Is it possible for God to lie? No! Is it possible for the Father to break His promise? No! Yet beyond the integrity of God, there is a greater reason why we can trust in the promise of a circumcised heart.

As we learned earlier, the Father has created us to share His love for Jesus. We can absolutely trust God's promise of circumcision, not simply because the Father loves us, but because He longs to love Jesus *through* us. Our selfish nature blocks this flow of love and so the Father will do anything to completely remove it. Just think: If the Father was to leave us with the blockage of the selfish nature, He would be denying Jesus a measure of His love. This can never happen! On the contrary, the Father's devotion to loving Jesus through us is so intense that He will do whatever it takes to make us pure channels of His love for Jesus. And He will do it as quickly as possible.

This makes the circumcision of the heart more than a promise. **It is a guaranteed reality for anyone who will pursue a life of wholehearted love.** The same God who went to such extreme lengths at the cross to overcome sin, is now equally ready to overcome sin *in us*. It is His work and so God is not calling us to look back at the finished work of the cross and try to make it real in our lives. He is calling us to look at Him right now and to trust Him to unleash the devastating power of the cross upon all our sin.

Throughout this process, we need to be careful to keep our vision set on the wholehearted love of Christ. This is always God's ultimate goal for us and it is the reason Jesus takes away our sin. When we make the first command our first priority, we activate God's promise to circumcise our hearts. Our faith gives the Father permission to put the scalpel to our hearts and cut away the cancer of the old self. Having circumcised the old self, the Father can then fill our hearts with His love for Jesus and help us to put on the new self, which is "putting on Christ."[6] As we become more one with Christ, Jesus can then love the Father with all His heart, soul, mind and strength through us.

Through the cross, we are blessed beyond imagination to become a part of the divine flow of love. The Father shares His love for Jesus with us, and Jesus pours out His love for the Father through us. This is the perfect plan of creation. It is God's amazing design and the only place we can find the reality of abundant life, extreme joy, and ultimate fulfilment. This is His goal, His design, His promise, and command. And it is all to His great delight and glory.

Pray

Father, thank you for offering to share your love for Jesus with me. Please give me the faith and hunger to devote myself to loving you with all my heart and soul. I want to be a pure channel of your love, free from every blockage of sin and selfishness. I invite you to go to the root of sin within me and remove everything in my life that is not of you. Thank you that I don't have to try to make this happen, but that you are able, you are faithful, and you will do it.

***

Note

In terms of clarity, it is important to know that Scripture often uses a variety of terms to refer to the same spiritual reality. The gift of salvation is referred to as being born again, as being redeemed, purchased, as coming to life from death, being brought out of darkness to light and so on. In the same way, Scripture refers to removal of the flesh nature in different ways. In Romans it is being crucified with Christ and being united in His death. In Colossians it is being circumcised in Christ and laying off the old self. In Matthew it is called the baptism of fire. As we go through the next few chapters, we will use all these terms to refer to the same experience: the complete removal of the flesh nature through the power of the cross.

Study Guide: page 200

11 | No Other Saviour

I sat in the office of a leader of the church I was attending. I had been running a Bible study during the year for university students, and in the last study we focused on the circumcision of the heart. After hearing about the study, he asked me to meet with him and then explained how the leadership did not believe that the circumcision of the heart was possible in this life.

"You can't teach these things here," he said. He seemed sincerely concerned. I listened and felt a genuine affection for him, but I also had a firm conviction regarding the reality of circumcision.

"Well, can I ask—is it because God cannot circumcise our hearts or because He doesn't want to?" I was met with silence. He simply stared into my eyes as both of us waited. I continued, "Because I believe that God loves us enough to want to remove the selfish nature from our hearts and that He is powerful enough to do it."

He sadly remained unmoved.

The sinful nature represents Satan's ultimate claim on a person's life and so he fiercely fights to keep his nature within people. Even in many churches, deceiving spirits influence teachers to twist Scripture and to teach man-made traditions as if they were God's truth.[1] Such teachings may sound biblical, but if they do not help us to enter our design of love and unity with God, they are either a distraction or a deception. True teaching will always put the first command in first place and empower people to grow in their love for Jesus. As Paul writes: the goal of our teaching is love from a pure heart. We need to judge *every* teaching by this standard of love and purity.[2]

In *Bride Arise*, we learned how the enemy uses two key strategies to rob people of their inheritance. The first is to teach believers that a certain part of their inheritance is not available in this life. The second strategy is to convince people that they have already possessed it. If a person believes either lie, they will naturally not seek to possess that part of their inheritance.

In terms of the first strategy, one of the most common distortions of the cross is that the blood of Jesus was not powerful enough to remove our sin. Instead, we are only truly set free from the sinful nature when we physically die. Few leaders teach this in plain terms, yet it is implied with every sermon that speaks of a never-ending struggle against sin. The unspoken message of this teaching is that we should expect and accept sinful desires for the rest of our lives.

Every teaching needs to be firmly founded upon the truth of Scripture. However, when we search for Scriptures that say we are set free from sin when we physically die, we find there are none. Not a single one. The Bible never says that we must continue to live with sin until we die, and it never says that the selfish nature is removed through physical death. As such, this doctrine has no Scriptural basis *at all*.

Deliverance Through Death

Isaiah 43:11

I am the LORD, and besides me there is no saviour.

If we believe that we are only fully saved from our sin nature at the point of our physical death, then we must also believe that death itself is our ultimate saviour. But is there any saviour other than God? No! Does Scripture ever speak of death as a source of salvation? No! Death is not a saviour, but an enemy that Jesus defeated at the cross.[3] On this subject, Adam Clarke writes:

> They hold out death as the complete deliverer from all corruption and the final destroyer of sin as if it were revealed in every page of the Bible! Whereas there is not one passage in the sacred volume that says any such thing! Were this true, then death, far from being the last enemy, would be the last and best friend, and the greatest of all deliverers. The truth is, death is neither the cause nor the means of destruction of sin. It is the blood of Jesus alone that cleanses from all unrighteousness.[4]

If we want to trust death for our deliverance and pretend that it is a second and greater saviour than Jesus, then we also must believe:
- That the blood of Jesus was not sufficient to remove the sin nature [5]
- That Jesus died for forgiveness but not for deliverance from sin [6]
- That Jesus did not take the full judgment of God upon sin at the cross [7]
- That sin is a physical condition, connected to our physical bodies [8]
- That Adam's fall was simply too great for the redemptive power of the blood of Jesus [9]
- That Jesus did not fully destroy the works of the enemy [10]
- That Jesus did not completely break the curse of sin at the cross [11]
- That Scripture is not entirely trustworthy or true [12]
- That Jesus was mistaken when He said, "It is finished." [13]
- That God *wants* the sinful nature to remain in us [14]

Dying Daily

1 Corinthians 15:31 (NASB)
I affirm, brethren, by the boasting in you which I have in Christ Jesus our Lord, I die daily.

In defence of the sinful-for-life teaching, some people say that Scripture calls us to put the selfish nature to death every day, until finally it dies when we physically die.

In 1 Corinthians 15, Paul is writing about how our faith is futile without the resurrection of Christ. If Jesus did not rise from the dead, then no one will rise after they physically die. Paul asks, if there was no resurrection then why would he willingly risk death every day? In effect Paul writes, "We are suffering and in danger every hour; indeed, I face death daily. Without the hope of resurrection, what is the point in fighting wild animals and risking our lives? For if the dead do not rise, let us eat and drink and enjoy life, for without resurrection we have no hope for a life beyond death."

Paul is writing of dying daily in terms of facing physical death every day. This is also clear in 1 Corinthians 4:9-13, Romans 8:35-37, 2 Corinthians 1:8-11, and 2 Corinthians 11:23-29. Combined these passages read:

> "God has exhibited us apostles as men condemned to death, who carry within ourselves the sentence of death, so that we would not trust in ourselves, but in God who raises the dead. For we are often in danger of death, and for your sake we are being put to death all day long. I have been beaten countless times, five times I've been lashed 39 times, beaten with rods, stoned, shipwrecked, nearly drowned, without sleep or food, cold and exposed, despairing even of life. But we have set our hope upon God who has delivered us from so great a peril of death, and will again deliver us."

Whenever Paul speaks of facing physical death, he uses the present tense ("I die daily"; "We are being put to death all day long.") However, when writing of the death of the selfish nature, Paul changes his tone dramatically. Instead of using the present tense, Paul uses the aorist, which represents a completed action. Alternatively, he uses the perfect tense, which describes an action that is "completed in the past, once and for all, not needing to be repeated, with a focus on the results of that action."[15] This is seen in Galatians 5:24, Romans 6:1-7, Galatians 2:20, Galatians 6:14, and Colossians 2:11. Combined these passages read:

> "Those in Christ Jesus *have* crucified the sin nature with all its passions and desires; for if we *have been* united with Him in His death then our old self *was* crucified with Him, so that our sin nature would be done away with, and we would no longer be slaves of sin. In Him we *were* circumcised by the removal of the flesh nature. Indeed, I *have been* crucified with Christ; it is no longer I that live but Christ that lives in me. And as such, I will boast only in the cross of our Lord Jesus Christ through which the world *has been* crucified to me, and I to the world."

Paul did not believe that we crucify the selfish nature each day, only to have it resurrect itself overnight.[16] Instead, he believed in the power of the cross to completely remove the flesh nature in this life *through faith.*[17] Jesus died for this. He took our sin nature into death at the cross so that we could be free to love Him with all our heart and soul. God has promised to do it, He is able to do it, and if we are willing, He will do it!

Overcoming the Fear

Most people refuse to believe that God removes the sinful nature because they want to justify a measure of sin in their lives. *We all have our vices; after all, we are only human.* So they use Bible verses to justify sin. *The heart is deceitfully wicked.*[18] *We all stumble in many ways.*[19] Paul was the foremost sinner.[20] Jesus teaches us to pray for forgiveness every day, so we must sin every day.[21] Romans says that the ongoing battle against the flesh is a part of our normal life.[22] John writes that we are deceiving ourselves if we say we have no sin.[23] Who can say they have made their heart pure?[24] No one! No one can say they are sinless or perfect!

Is Christ our salvation? Yes! Is He our redemption? Yes! Is Jesus our righteousness? Yes! And is Jesus our perfection?

Many people reject the circumcision of the heart because they equate it with reaching a state of *sinless perfection*. To these people, the term *sinless perfection* is a state of immunity to all sin and temptation, and of complete spiritual maturity with no need for further spiritual growth.

This is not what the circumcision of the heart implies at all. Jesus Himself was tempted in every way, and each temptation was authentic.[25] He had no sinful nature within Him, but still He felt, suffered and battled through every temptation. Jesus felt lust and overcame it. He faced greed, pride, doubt, fear, envy, and hate and He overcame them all. Through these temptations Jesus learned obedience and He always found the grace to stand. This is how He can sympathise with us in our weaknesses in times of temptation—He has been there and experienced it all. He has overcome and now He offers His help in our time of need so that we can overcome with Him.

Therefore, the gift of circumcision does not mean that we will never again make mistakes, hurt people, believe a lie, or even sin against God. It does not mean that we cannot fall from grace or be deceived. It simply means that the selfish nature has been removed from our hearts and that every desire to sin is gone. In this place, we will still be subject to temptation. As we will see in future chapters, the enemy will still attack us in our thoughts and feelings. A spirit of pride may whisper subtle thoughts to us, attempting to take our focus off Jesus and steal our humility. A spirit of lust may attempt to twist our desire for intimacy and use it against us to sow lust into our hearts. While on this earth, there will always be temptations. Yet having been through the circumcision of the heart, we know that all these temptations will be coming from the external forces of darkness and the world, and not out of the fallen desires of our own flesh. Knowing the source of the feelings and thoughts, we can respond in authority and shut down the attack.

If for any reason, we give into a temptation, we must be quick to acknowledge it, confess it, and let the blood of Jesus completely wash it away. If we do not, we risk allowing the enemy to sow seeds of the sinful nature back into our hearts. We must be quick to recognise these attacks in their infancy and overcome every one.

In terms of the word *perfection*, the Bible often speaks of perfection, but not in the same sense as the modern English word. We are called to pursue perfection in the sense of completeness and maturity, which we find in unity with Jesus. This is not the perfection of having reached a state where no more growth is possible.[26] Such a state does not exist for us, for the love of Christ is infinite and we can always grow deeper into His love. John Wesley gives his perspective, writing:

> "What is, then, the perfection of which man is capable, while he dwells in a corruptible body? It is the complying with that kind command: 'My son, give me thy heart.' It is the 'loving the Lord his God with all his heart, and with all his soul, and with all his mind.' This is the sum of Christian perfection: it is comprised in that one word; love."[27]

Ultimately, the idea that we can never be free from sin in this life denies the all-loving and all-powerful nature of God. It says that God does not remove the sinful nature from our hearts in our lifetime, but it fails to say *why*. Why does God wait until death to save us? Is it because He cannot remove the sinful nature from us in this life? Or is it because He does not want to?

Neither of these is true. For Scripture reveals a God for whom all things are possible, a God who passionately loves people and died to set us free from our sin. If we would devote ourselves to a life of love, we would quickly discover that not only can God remove our selfish nature, but that He truly wants to. The Father is passionate about removing every barrier to His design of love in our lives.

So what is the main consequence of believing that Jesus can circumcise the sin nature from our hearts and empower us to love Him with all our heart? Surely it is that we pursue a life of wholehearted love and unity with Him.

But what are the consequences of believing that we are only set free from sin when we die? Surely it is that we do not pursue a wholehearted love for Jesus, nor do we experience the circumcision of the heart. Surely it is that we deny our design and the power of the cross, and instead, we experience a lifetime of struggle against sin—just as we believed we would.

The stakes are too high to get this wrong. Let us put our trust in our God of Love, who alone can make His design of love a reality in us. He is able and He is good. He will do it.

Pray

Holy Spirit, I give you permission to remove every barrier to your love in my life. Please take all my old ways of thinking, my faulty theologies, and corrupt mindsets. Please remove the lies and assumptions and let your truth be written on my heart. Reveal your truth to me and lead me into reality.

12 | Everything Already

Romans 6:5-7
For if we have been united with him in a death like his, we shall certainly be united with him in a resurrection like his. We know that our old self was crucified with him in order that the body of sin might be brought to nothing, so that we would no longer be enslaved to sin. For one who has died has been set free from sin.

The prevailing flawed theology concerning the selfish nature is that it only dies when we physically die. However, in recent times, another theology has been taking ground, which we refer to as the "Everything-Already" teaching. This teaching references passages such as Roman 6 where Paul writes that "our old self *was* crucified with Him." It teaches that the selfish nature was removed when we first believed in Jesus (or were baptised in water). In other words, the moment we first turned to Jesus in repentance, God cut away the old self without us realising it.

The obvious problem with this teaching is that everyone still experiences sinful instincts *after* they start to follow Jesus. So how can the selfish nature be removed and yet its selfish desires still remain? This teaching says that the reason people still struggle with sin is not because the sinful nature is still alive within them, but because they are believing a lie. If people would truly believe in what God has done for them, they would have no desire to sin.

Bound by Agreement

In the spiritual realm, everything happens through agreement. The Spirit of God does not force us to receive any of His blessings. Why? Because grace must always be freely given and freely received. This is particularly true for the gift of love. The moment we try to force someone to receive our love, it is no longer love. Therefore, even though God longs to cut away all our sin and flood us with His affection, He must wait for our agreement.

> **1 Corinthians 3:1-3**
> But I, brothers, could not address you as spiritual people, but as people of the flesh, as infants in Christ. I fed you with milk, not solid food, for you were not ready for it. And even now you are not yet ready, for you are still of the flesh. For while there is jealousy and strife among you, are you not of the flesh and behaving only in a human way?

In this passage, Paul equates being "infants in Christ" with being "people of the flesh." Paul wanted to talk to the Corinthian believers as spiritual adults, but instead, he could only feed them milk because they still lived according to their selfish nature rather than the Spirit. Their agreement with their flesh prevented God from circumcising their hearts and left them trapped in a place of spiritual infancy.

This principle of agreement is one of the key reasons why God rarely circumcises the heart when a person first starts to follow Jesus. When most of us give our lives to Christ, we keep a level of agreement with our selfish nature. We do not come to Him pursuing a life of wholehearted love. Many of us come to faith simply to secure a life in heaven after we die. In our infancy, we still want to live for ourselves. We agree with our selfishness. We agree with our pride, lust and greed. And God does not overrule these agreements. He allows our selfish nature to remain because we allow it.

Because the sinful nature is still alive within us, our spiritual infancy is usually defined by a cycle of sin, repentance and forgiveness. As our loving Father, God continually forgives the selfish behaviour of our youth, but He also constantly calls us to press on to maturity. To help us to spiritually mature, the Holy Spirit speaks to us about our design of love. He helps us to discover who we are in Christ and to forge an identity with Him, free from the selfish nature. We soon come to see the first command as the first promise, and we receive the faith we need from the Spirit to pursue a life of wholehearted love. We realise that this is what we were created for—our whole being was perfectly made to thrive in love.

When we make a covenant to love God with all our heart, soul, mind and strength, we enter into the highest form of agreement. This gives God the permission He needs to make us selfless through the removal of the selfish nature. Leaning on God's grace, we can then break all agreements with our flesh nature and seek to be crucified with Christ. And of course, with great joy, God is faithful to make it our reality.

Specific Faith

It is essential that we understand the role of faith in our spiritual growth. If we do not have faith to receive the gift of forgiveness, we will not experience the awesome liberty of being free from all guilt and shame. Likewise, if we do not believe that God truly loves us, we will not be able to recognise or receive the gift of His love. In the same way, we cannot experience the circumcision of the heart unless we have faith specifically for circumcision.

As mentioned earlier, there are people who believe that because Paul writes that "our old self *was* crucified with Him," the use of the past tense means that all believers have already been crucified with Christ, regardless of whether they believe it or not. However, it is important to see how Paul's writings are shaped by the constraints of the Greek language in which the aorist and present forms speak more of the nature (aspect) of an action than its timing (tense). The aorist refers to a completed action and the Greek present speaks of an ongoing action. If Paul were to write in the present tense, it would imply that being crucified with Christ is an ongoing, continual, or habitual action. Because it is a spiritual experience that happens at a point in time in the life of a believer, Paul rightly chooses to use the aorist form. However, when this is translated into the English past tense, confusion can arise for some people.[1]

It is important to see that Paul's goal in the book of Romans is not to state that all believers are already crucified with Christ in actual experience, otherwise there would be no need to write about it. Instead, Paul is revealing the awesome power of the cross and inviting people to let Jesus destroy the old self. He presents the cross like a gift that God has already given us, but one that can make no difference in our lives if it remains unopened on the table. Each one of us needs to receive the gift and access the power of the cross *through specific faith*. And it is essential that we do this because we can never love God with our entire being while the selfish nature possesses any part of us. We must allow the cross to remove our old nature so that we can live in God's design of wholehearted love.[2]

Inheritance and Possession

Colossians 3:9-11

Do not lie to one another, seeing that you have put off the old self with its practices and have put on the new self, which is being renewed in knowledge after the image of its creator. Here there is not Greek and Jew, circumcised and uncircumcised, barbarian, Scythian, slave, free; but Christ is all, and in all.

Ephesians 4:20-24

But that is not the way you learned Christ!— assuming that you have heard about him and were taught in him, as the truth is in Jesus, to put off your old self, which belongs to your former manner of life and is corrupt through deceitful desires, and to be renewed in the spirit of your minds, and to put on the new self, created after the likeness of God in true righteousness and holiness.

By saying that the work of circumcision is already finished for all believers, the Everything-Already teaching confuses the concepts of inheritance and possession. Our inheritance is everything that God has given us in Christ Jesus. Our possession is what we spiritually experience right now. For example, in these passages, Paul writes that we "have put off the old self," but then he calls us to "put off the old self." If all believers put off the old self when they first believed, why would Paul call us to do something that has already taken place?

The truth is that the first passage speaks of our inheritance in the cross to free us from our old self. The second passage then invites us to access our inheritance by faith and make it our possession through personal experience.

When we understand the difference between inheritance and possession, we start to see the problems of the Everything-Already doctrine. If all believers are already crucified with Christ, then everyone is already loving God with all their heart and soul. Is this what we experience in our own lives? Is this what we see in others? And if this were true, why would Scripture constantly command us to love? The fact is that we all need to take a journey into our inheritance of love.

A New Legalism
John 16:13a
"But when He, the Spirit of truth [reality], comes, He will guide you into all the truth [reality]…

A key problem with the Everything-Already teaching is that it quietly denies the role of the Holy Spirit in taking us into reality. It says, *God has already crucified your old self! Your fear, your lust, your pride and greed—it has all been taken away already! The Scripture says so. You just have to believe it. If you are struggling with sin or selfishness, it is because you're not believing the truth. If you would only believe, it would become a reality for you. Try harder to believe.*

At its foundation, the Everything-Already teaching is built on the idea that our belief creates reality.[3] This kind of teaching compels people to strive in their own strength to believe rather than trust in the Holy Spirit to bring us into reality. So people memorise Scripture, recite, pray and declare the word of God, but they still fail to overcome their selfish instincts.

The result is that this teaching becomes just another form of legalism, one which weighs people down with a burden of belief that is impossible to bear and then blames them for their failure. Apart from Christ, no one can intellectually believe their way into salvation, healing, freedom, the baptism of the Holy Spirit, the circumcision of the heart, or any other blessing of God. They are all gifts that come *from* God. And because they are gifts of His grace, we can never earn them, not even by spiritual practices such as prayer, fasting or declaration.

Yes, we participate with God through faith, but this faith is not the same as self-generated belief. Self-generated belief comes from our own mind as we try to talk ourselves into the truth. In contrast, real faith is the confidence that we receive from God when the Holy Spirit speaks to us. This confidence allows us to access God's grace without striving, which in turn allows the Holy Spirit to make His gifts a reality in our lives. In this way, Jesus offers us His yoke so that He can bear our entire burden, from faith to belief to action. This is His job and joy! The Spirit of Jesus loves to tell us about what is to come and give us the faith we need to receive God's grace. He loves to make our inheritance real for us and then energise us to act in love. No doctrine can ever replace Him, and our ability to believe will never begin to match the power of His faith. If we want to experience true freedom in Christ, we simply need to hear His voice, share His faith, and trust Him to lead us into reality. And He will do it because He is an eternally loving, infinitely good, completely faithful, promise-keeping God!

Truly Free

One woman who was shaped by the Everything-Already stream of belief shared her experience with me. She never felt that she could be honest about what was happening in her heart, not even with God. She could feel the selfishness of her flesh nature rage within her, but she believed that it was only happening because she was failing to believe the truth. Because of this teaching, she felt that it would be an act of unbelief to even acknowledge the presence of her selfish instincts. So she would deny what was happening in her heart and instead strive for a better belief.

For this woman, God's design of wholehearted love and the promise of the circumcision of the heart was not just good news. It was awesome news! She was overwhelmed with relief and as the tears flowed, she was filled with hope. She could now be honest with God and trust in Him to keep His promise. She started to share with God about her struggle with selfishness and she began to hear His voice more clearly. He never called her to try to believe harder. Instead, He simply lavished her with love and assured her that He could circumcise her heart. He was always supremely confident in His own ability to set her free. He was both willing and able. Her only work was to fall into His arms and say, *Yes*.

Pray

Father, I thank you for all the good gifts you have given me—more than I could ever think of or imagine. You are better than anyone has ever dreamed. Please help me to become so completely confident in your goodness that I would never hesitate to receive a gift from you. I thank you for the gift of sharing your love for Jesus. I surrender to it. Please circumcise my heart and take me into your promise of a wholehearted love. I love you!

13 | Waves Rise Up

Galatians 5:22-24
But the fruit of the Spirit is love, joy, peace, patience, kindness, goodness, faithfulness, gentleness, self-control; against such things there is no law. And those who belong to Christ Jesus have crucified the flesh with its passions and desires.

When we set our face towards the cross, the enemy responds. He will do anything to distract us or sow doubt regarding the power of the cross. Many readers may have even found it a battle to read this book. But battle we must. The kingdom of God and its design of wholehearted love is taken by force, and it is a fight to the death.

As we have seen, the first strategy the enemy generally uses against us is to tempt us to believe that it is not attainable. When that fails, he will then try to make us strive to attain a circumcised heart in our own strength. As part of our pursuit of love, we must be prepared to face both attacks.

Standing Firm

Often when people learn about the circumcision of the heart, it challenges what they have believed about sin, their identity, and the power of the cross. But instead of asking the Holy Spirit and searching the Scriptures, they look to see what respected Christians believe about the circumcision of the heart. This can often be the first point of challenge.

There are leaders all over the world who are genuinely trying to serve the Lord, but who do not believe in the circumcision of the heart. They are doing their best with what they know, but they have not yet learned to put the first command into first place. Maybe they are yet to get a revelation of the cross and their design of love. Maybe they have doubt or fear. Maybe they have never questioned or tested the traditional teaching about freedom from sin.

For some people, dying to self can seem too costly or painful to accept. As such, some people, including leaders and even famous Christians, adopt a theology to justify the presence of sin in their hearts. This theology is like saying, "Cancer is normal; everyone has it. But praise God, when we die, we will be free from our cancer to live forever with Christ." Such a theology blinds people to the problem of sin and the cure of the cross.

The ultimate tragedy here is that the cost is an illusion. Compared to the prize, there is no cost. We give our lives to Christ and He sets us free from the cancer of selfishness so that we can experience abundant life before we physically die. Where is the cost? Is it not only our sin? Jesus demands that we give Him the corruption and death that we carry in our hearts, and in our fallen thinking we call this a cost too high? The only true cost of the cross was paid by Jesus in blood. For everyone else, the cross holds only the gift of the life of Christ, which is far more precious than any sacrifice.

Ultimately, the greatest cost will be felt by those that do not give up their sin and selfish nature, even if they are famous leaders. Such people hold fast to their cancer in the face of the cure. They carry the cost with them, every day to their death, unknowingly dishonouring the cross, denying their design of love, and rejecting the grace of God.

Waiting for Permission

Next we must face the temptation to try to kill our selfish nature in our own strength. This is futile, as flesh will never overcome flesh. God alone can do it. Because He has infinite power, it is as easy for God to circumcise our hearts as it is for Him to forgive us. God is not waiting until He has the strength or inclination to remove our selfish nature, He is waiting for our permission.

In our natural mind, the idea of loving God with all our heart and soul is something completely impossible. This makes it difficult to have a vision for wholehearted love let alone give God permission to make it a reality. The natural mind cannot look past its own limitations to see a God who is infinite in both love and power. But God is good. He will meet us where we are and lead us on. So if we are struggling to believe, we can present our unbelief to God and ask for His help. He will then speak to us and share His faith with us. This is something He would love to do. We simply need to ask.

Storms Arise
God longs to bring us to the end of ourselves so that He can be fully free to bring us into our design. For many people, this process can mean facing a storm.

> **Mark 4:35-41**
> On that day, when evening had come, he said to them, "Let us go across to the other side." And leaving the crowd, they took him with them in the boat, just as he was. And other boats were with him. And a great windstorm arose, and the waves were breaking into the boat, so that the boat was already filling. But he was in the stern, asleep on the cushion. And they woke him and said to him, "Teacher, do you not care that we are perishing?" And he awoke and rebuked the wind and said to the sea, "Peace! Be still!" And the wind ceased, and there was a great calm. He said to them, "Why are you so afraid? Have you still no faith?" And they were filled with great fear and said to one another, "Who then is this, that even the wind and the sea obey him?"

After sharing many parables with the people, Jesus asked His disciples to sail across the lake. During the night, a storm rose up and threatened to overwhelm the boat. While the disciples fought against the storm, Jesus slept. Fearing for their lives, the disciples cried out to Jesus and He spoke and calmed the storm. The disciples were amazed and asked, "Who is this?"

The calming of the storm follows a series of parables and is itself a living parable—an actual event that communicates a revelation of God. In order to understand the parable, we need to ask some questions of the Spirit of God.

Why did Jesus sleep through such a great storm? Where did the storm come from? And why did the disciples fear for their lives?

> **Psalm 107:23-31** (NASB)
> Those who go down to the sea in ships,
>   who do business on great waters;
> they have seen the works of the LORD,
>   and His wonders in the deep.
> For He spoke and raised up a stormy wind,
>   which lifted up the waves of the sea.
> They rose up to the heavens, they went down to the depths;
>   their soul melted away in their misery.
> they reeled and staggered like a drunken man,
>   and were at their wits' end.
> Then they cried to the LORD in their trouble,
>   and He brought them out of their distresses.
> He caused the storm to be still,
>   so that the waves of the sea were hushed.
> Then they were glad because they were quiet,
>   so He guided them to their desired haven.
> Let them give thanks to the LORD for His lovingkindness,
>   and for His wonders to the sons of men!

When they crossed the lake, the disciples sailed straight into a divine storm. On the surface it looked like a disaster. Yet God had raised up the storm for His purposes. He was not seeking glory but showing His loving-kindness by bringing the disciples to the end of themselves.

The storm revealed the unbelief and fear in the hearts of the disciples. They cried out to Jesus, who then calmed the storm. Surely the disciples remembered Psalm 107. Surely they remembered that only God calms the seas. Who then is this, that even the wind and sea obey him? It is the Creator God, living through His Son, Jesus Christ.

Like the disciples, in order to reach our desired haven of wholehearted love, we need to come to the end of ourselves. This can be a terrifying part of the journey. But we need to become so desperate to be free of our old self that we are willing to cry out to the Lord in our distress. He will then hear us and calm our storms. He will circumcise our hearts and lead us safely to a land of wholehearted love.

First Steps

Our first step into the blessing of circumcision is to accept that we cannot earn it, we cannot believe our way into it, and we cannot pretend that it has already happened. We need to recognise that only the Holy Spirit can release the power of the cross into our lives. Our second step is to devote our lives to the wholehearted love of God. I can remember praying, *"God, I give myself—everything I am and everything I have—to loving you. I give you my whole heart, and those parts of my heart that I can't give, I ask you to take anyway. Consume me with your love."* This was not a one-time prayer. It was part of a process of becoming truly devoted to the first command.

This prayer provided me with a defence while I was still struggling with indwelling sin. I had often imagined what the Father would ask me when I arrived in eternity. All I could imagine Him asking me was, "How much do you love My Son?" I could not bear the thought of saying anything less than "I love Him with all my heart, soul, mind and strength." I had to be able to say this truthfully, but I knew it was impossible on my own. So my defence in eternity would be my devotion to love in this life. Then I could appear before the Father and say, "I wanted to love Jesus with all my heart and soul, and in fact, I devoted my entire life to it, but You did not circumcise my heart as You had promised." This conversation of course can never happen. It is utterly impossible for God to break His promise to circumcise the heart of someone who is truly devoted to the first command. As people used to say: Entire sanctification comes with entire consecration. If we are wholly devoted to loving God, as surely as the Father loves Jesus, He will keep His promise to us. It is guaranteed.

Time to Take Responsibility
Ecclesiastes 3:1
For everything there is a season, and a time for every matter under heaven.

There is a perfect time for everything, including a time to die. If we want to be crucified with Christ, the Holy Spirit will make it a reality, but He will do it in His perfect time. So right now, ask the Holy Spirit which part of your inheritance He is leading you into. Is it time to grow in the blessings of strength, peace, joy, or humility? Is it time to get to know Jesus as your Friend or Bridegroom? Is it time simply to rest in the Father's embrace? Or is it finally time to know Jesus as your Sanctifier, the One who circumcises your heart?

If now is your time to be crucified with Christ, get ready for the waves to rise up. The Spirit will begin to expose the flesh as He separates it from the real you. Things will become intense for a season, and you will probably feel more sinful than ever. As the sin rises up, confess it to God. If you have someone who is also on the journey into wholehearted love, feel free to confess it to them too. Acknowledge that by yielding to your sin nature, you have allowed it to bring spiritual death into the world. Take full responsibility for its effects. Having confessed your sin, access the power of the blood of Jesus to break the effects of your sinful actions by praying something like:

> *Father, I thank you that you have completely defeated death through Jesus. You are awesome. In Jesus' name, with the power and authority of His life in me, I now break the works of my sinful flesh over myself. I break the power of every word and work of my flesh with respect to my parents, my family, my friends, and everyone else who has received death at my hand. These words and works, and any curses they have brought, are now totally destroyed through the power of the blood of Jesus and the authority of His name.*

Father, I pray that where the work of the flesh has brought death and wounding to myself or others, that you would release life and healing, completely undoing every effect of my sin and selfishness.

I now break my covenant with my selfish nature. It is not me. I break every agreement with it, fully cancelling any permission I have given it to remain in my life. I declare that it will die at the cross and I will rise with Christ. Jesus, I will be one with You and together we will love the Father with all our heart, soul, mind, and strength. We will be one in wholehearted, selfless love. This is Your will, and I fully agree with it. Let Your will be done. May this be to Your glory and great delight. You are my love!

Now ask the Holy Spirit if there is anyone that you need to reconcile with. Seek forgiveness from anyone you have hurt or who has anything against you. Make amends as the Spirit leads. It will be humbling, perhaps even painful at times. But it will be worth it. It will completely strip the flesh of its power over you. And in a little while, you will be crucified with Christ and raised to a life of wholehearted love. He is calling.

14 | Not I but Christ

"I am the only one to blame for this.
   Somehow it all turns out the same.
   Soaring on the wings of selfish pride, I flew too high,
   And like Icarus, I collide.

"With a world I try so hard to leave behind,
   To rid myself of all but love,
   To give and die.

"All said and done I stand alone,
   Amongst the remains of a life I should not own.
   It takes all I am to believe,
   In the mercy that covers me."

          - "Worlds Apart" by Jars of Clay

The words of this song echoed through my mind as I sat on the floor of my bedroom. I was excelling at university, but only because I was working to escape the pain. I had been living life my own way without realising that in my pursuit of worldly pleasure, I was trading away all joy. The life had drained from my soul and I quickly found myself in a place of complete spiritual desolation.

For months, I refused to talk to God, not feeling worthy enough to raise my eyes to Him. My only prayer was at the end of each day: *May Your unfailing love come to me; Your salvation according to Your promise.*[1]

Finally, I sat on the floor and realised that as the captain of my soul, I had led myself straight onto the rocks. I sat in the ruins of my shipwrecked life as the waves continued to crash over me. I admitted defeat, honestly wishing that I could be anyone else in the world other than me. Then the words of this song came to my mind and I realised: My life is not my own. I had stolen it away from the One who had purchased me, and it was finally time to give it back.

The next few months were a time of restoration. I was determined to disown my life and let God take over. Galatians 2:20 became my goal.

> **Galatians 2:20**
> I have been crucified with Christ. It is no longer I who live, but Christ who lives in me. And the life I now live in the flesh [body] I live by faith in the Son of God, who loved me and gave himself for me.

For Paul, the power of the cross was not a theory or theology. It was reality. Paul's testimony became my promise. I cried out to God that it may be no longer I who live. The words of an old hymn became my constant prayer.

> Not I, but Christ be honoured, loved, exalted,
> Not I, but Christ be seen, be known and heard;
> Not I, but Christ in every look and action,
> Not I, but Christ in every thought and word.
>
> Not I, but Christ to gently soothe in sorrow,
> Not I, but Christ to wipe the falling tear;
> Not I, but Christ to lift the weary burden,
> Not I, but Christ to hush away all fear.
>
> Not I, but Christ, in lowly, silent labour;
> Not I, but Christ, in humble, earnest toil;
> Christ, only Christ—no show, no ostentation;
> Christ, none but Christ, the gath'rer of the spoil.
>
> Christ, only Christ, no idle word e'er falling,
> Christ, only Christ, no needless bustling sound;
> Christ, only Christ, no self-important bearing,
> Christ, only Christ, no trace of I be found.

> Christ, only Christ, ere long will fill my vision,
> Glory excelling; soon, full soon I'll see;
> Christ, only Christ, my every wish fulfilling,
> Christ, only Christ, my all in all to be.
>
> Oh, to be saved from myself, dear Lord,
> Oh, to be lost in Thee!
> Oh, that it may be no more I,
> But Christ that lives in me.

God began to answer my prayer. It was not long before He led me to the promise of the first command. I knew I could not keep it myself, so I placed my trust in God to make it a reality. At this stage, I had not yet discovered Deuteronomy 30:6 and the promise of a circumcised heart. I simply knew that God would not command me to do anything that He could not do through me. So I devoted my life to keeping the first command and asked Him to take over. This devotion to love led me on a journey to make a covenant of love with God and discover Jesus as my bridegroom. We look at this more in *Bride Arise*. Not long later, it led me to experience Jesus as the one who puts the axe to the root and takes away all sin.

Freedom in Death

For some reason, I grew up believing that God would only remove the sinful nature from my heart when I physically died. I did not hear anyone specifically preach this, but it seemed to permeate every message: life is all about striving against sin, but when we die, we will be free from sin in heaven. So I kept striving against sin, only to fail over and over.

I longed to be free from the sinful nature long before I ever believed it was possible. I remember lying on my bed during my first year at university, imagining what it would be like to die. I imagined bullets ripping through me and feeling only one thing: relief. At last, I would die. At last, I would be free from all the pride and lust and insecurity. At last, I would be free from the torment of my sinful nature.

It never occurred to me that the Bible never speaks of physical death as being our deliverer from sin. My fantasies of death were based on the lie that my final enemy was actually some kind of saviour. I was living in unbelief and idolatry, attributing to physical death the glory of a salvation that was only purchased by the blood of Jesus.

As we saw earlier, there is no Scripture that says we are crucified with Christ at the point of physical death. It is a gift of God's grace that we experience in this present life. If the flesh nature is only cut away by physical death, then salvation would be attained by a work which is void of faith. For no one needs faith to die; it simply happens. For salvation from indwelling sin to be a free gift of grace, it has to be able to be experienced by faith alone. This means that it must be available now.

Under Attack

I had devoted my life to wholehearted love, which gave God permission to prepare me for circumcision. The first step was to separate my identity from the selfish nature. God helped me to do this in a surprising way.

I was standing in a church waiting on God in worship. The Holy Spirit opened my eyes to see myself clothed in the armour of light. I saw a great, full-length shield, held in place by my left hand and forearm. I looked down and I could see the dazzling breastplate of faith and love. Then suddenly, a flash of silver passed behind my shield and sliced through my armour, cutting deeply into my chest. In one motion it carved through my left-side ribs, slicing down into my abdomen. I started to collapse forward.

That has got to be fatal. I grabbed my stomach and tried to understand what had just happened. *Where did that come from?* I looked up but was then taken into a third-person perspective so I could see the scene from a different angle. I was next to the person who had struck me and could see myself standing in the distance, still clothed in the armour of light. The man next to me was dressed all in black and was holding a sword with an ivory-carved handle in his left hand. I looked at his face and saw myself. *It was me.*

"That is your flesh, and it is trying to kill you." The Spirit spoke and the vision ended.

The Holy Spirit used this vision to teach me who I was and who I was not. My old self embodied everything that was evil within my heart. All the rage, lust, pride, greed, selfish-ambition, rejection, insecurity and hatred I had been thinking was a part of me, was actually part of this evil called the flesh or sinful nature. Only now could I see how determined it was to destroy the real me.

Previously, in my religious legalism, I had made a treaty with my flesh. It could remain in my heart so long as it did not try to take over too much. I would tolerate an ongoing yet concealable level of lust and pride and be satisfied with the knowledge that the blood of Jesus had secured my forgiveness. After all, we are all only human right? Only now I had seen the nature of the beast. The treaty had to be cancelled. The old self had been warring against me the whole time, never bringing any blessing, just pain, addiction and devastation. How could I possibly carry on in partnership with such a desperately evil presence?

The Challenge

1 John 1:7-9

But if we walk in the light, as he is in the light, we have fellowship with one another, and the blood of Jesus his Son cleanses us from all sin. If we say we have no sin, we deceive ourselves, and the truth is not in us. If we confess our sins, he is faithful and just to forgive us our sins and to cleanse us from all unrighteousness.

Around this time, I was at a meeting when someone shared the power of the cross with me. They claimed that the blood of Jesus is sufficient to cleanse us from *all* sin. The blood is powerful enough to tear the selfish nature out of our hearts and to enable us to love God with all our hearts. But first we need to be willing to be crucified with Christ. We have to agree with God by turning against our selfish nature and asking God to circumcise it from our hearts.

After hearing about the power of the blood I was left conflicted. Could I dare to believe? Could this be true? It made sense that the sacrifice of Jesus was sufficient to take away my sin and free me from the torment of the old self. But I had always believed that it only happens when you die. Even though I had been praying that "it would be no longer I who live," I had not truly connected this prayer with being crucified with Christ! I was uncertain about it all, but I knew one thing for sure: God had brought me to the end of myself. I had seen what the old self is truly like and I could not continue living with it anymore. If I had to die to be free, then so be it.

"God, I've had enough. I want to be free. If I can only be free from my flesh through physical death then please, kill me physically. But if I can be free through some sort of spiritual death, then please, crucify me with you."

There was no response. I walked out of the church and onto the street and looked around. It was night. I drew a slow breath and honestly wondered if this would be my last night on earth.

Pray

Holy Spirit, I need you. I do not want to be in control of my own life anymore. I give you full permission to take over. I offer my body as a living sacrifice. I have been fully purchased and I now ask to be fully possessed by You. Help me to see the true nature of my flesh and to make it my enemy. Lead me to the cross and into your freedom. I know you can do this.

15 | Set Apart

1 Thessalonians 5:23
Now may the God of peace himself sanctify you completely, and may your whole spirit and soul and body be kept blameless at the coming of our Lord Jesus Christ. He who calls you is faithful; he will surely do it.

Sanctification
The generic meaning of sanctification is "the state of proper functioning." To sanctify someone or something is to set that person or thing apart for the use intended by its designer. A pen is "sanctified" when used to write. Eyeglasses are "sanctified" when used to improve sight. In the theological sense, things are sanctified when they are used for the purpose God intends. A human being is sanctified, therefore, when he or she lives according to God's design and purpose.[1]

The Greek word *hagiazo* (translated as *sanctify* or *make holy*) means to set something apart for its intended use. God sanctifies us and makes us His saints (*sanctified ones*) by restoring us to His design of wholehearted love and unity with Christ. This means that holiness is far more than not sinning; it is loving in unity with Jesus according to His design. This design requires both the removal of our flesh nature and the infilling of the nature of Christ.

The Holy Spirit is the *Spirit of Hagiazo*, given to restore our design of love and purity. To bring us into love, the Spirit makes us one with Him and fills us with the Father's love for Jesus. He then focuses on sanctification. This is entirely His work, but it requires both our permission and participation. As soon as we are truly willing, the Holy Spirit takes us on a journey to the cross to remove the sin nature. Along the journey, the Holy Spirit separates the light from the darkness within our own sense of identity. This separation ends our agreement with the flesh nature which allows God to sanctify us *completely*.

Off with the Old, On with the New
> Colossians 3:9-10
> Do not lie to one another, seeing that you have put off the old self with its practices and have put on the new self, which is being renewed in knowledge after the image of its Creator.

In Christ, we are a new creation, created in the image of God.[2] However, we cannot truly become this new creation until we put off our old self. To lay aside the old self means that we are to wholly separate ourselves from our selfish nature.

As we saw earlier, an essential part of this work of holiness is receiving the revelation that *we are not our old self*. It is not a part of us and so it must not define us. In practical terms, this means that we must separate our sense of identity from our sinful self and no longer think of ourselves as a mixture of both good and evil. In Christ, we are not evil. We are not lustful, vain, greedy or proud. We are not envious, insecure or fearful. We are not selfish or unkind. These are merely traits of the old self that distort our sense of identity. God created us and so He alone has the right to define our identity. And He says that we are created in the image of Christ. God says that we are created to be a channel of His love for Jesus and to live in unity with Him. Who are we to argue against our Designer?

When God gave me the vision of being attacked by my old self, it instantly helped me to separate my identity from the old self. I began to believe that the real me is only found in unity with Jesus. In fact, apart from Christ, there is no me. From that time on, I went to war with my flesh. It had to die.

Romans 6:1-7

What shall we say then? Are we to continue in sin that grace may abound? By no means! How can we who died to sin still live in it? Do you not know that all of us who have been baptised into Christ Jesus were baptised into his death? We were buried therefore with him by baptism into death, in order that, just as Christ was raised from the dead by the glory of the Father, we too might walk in newness of life.

For if we have been united with him in a death like his, we shall certainly be united with him in a resurrection like his. We know that our old self was crucified with him in order that the body of sin might be brought to nothing, so that we would no longer be enslaved to sin. For one who has died has been set free from sin.

Baptism is a total immersion to the point of saturation. When we are baptised in the Spirit, every part of our being is saturated with the Holy Spirit and we become one with Him. In the same way, when we are baptised into the death of Christ, every part of the selfish nature is immersed into death. *Every part.*

Crucifixion may be a slower death than others, but it is always sure. There is not a single record in ancient Rome of anyone surviving crucifixion. It always results in death in the natural realm, and the same is true spiritually. While there can be a process of crucifixion, it will not take forever. If we nail our flesh to the cross, it will certainly die. And just beyond death is the glory of a life of wholehearted love.

Many people believe that God can circumcise a person's heart in a single moment of faith. And this could well be true. In the natural realm, some people die instantly, while others spend years dying. For me it was a process that took some time. Many months after the first vision I was still struggling with my sinful instincts—greed, gluttony, pride, lust, apathy—it seemed like an endless and draining conflict. The sinful emotions and thoughts that would rise up within me seemed overpowering at times, but the blood of Christ was always more powerful. If I had hurt someone, I would try to make it right. Though it would ebb and flow, the conflict between spirit and flesh carried on every day. I tried to distract myself from it with work, but whenever I paused, I could sense sin boiling just below the surface, ready to erupt out and rain down its fire. All I could do was fix my eyes on the cross and keep going.

Come and Die

> "As we embark upon discipleship we surrender ourselves to Christ in union with his death—we give over our lives to death. Thus it begins; the cross is not the terrible end to an otherwise god-fearing and happy life, but it meets us at the beginning of our communion with Christ. When Christ calls a man, he bids him come and die...it is the same death every time—death in Jesus Christ, the death of the old man at his call."
>
> - Deitrich Bonhoeffer[3]

I was a part of a small group at the time and the Lord took us all on the journey into circumcision. We were all separating the sin nature from our own identity and learning not to relate to one another in the flesh, but to see others as who they truly were in Christ. This allowed us to confess our sin to one another without fear of any judgment, condemnation or shame. When sin rose up, we looked to the cross not just for forgiveness, but to have the sin completely cut out of our hearts. Jesus took away all the sin we gave Him, and we all became more and more free.

Over the course of several months, God revealed on two occasions that my old self was getting weaker and the real me was getting stronger. Then one day, I was praying with my small group and I knelt before God. He took me into a vision so real that I could almost feel what was happening to me.[4]

The vision started with the feeling of gravel pressing into the side of my cheek. I realised that my head was being crushed into the ground. Across my shoulders was the crossbar of a cross which weighed 300-400kgs (800lbs). I lay pinned to the ground and my heart sank. For months I had been seeking to be crucified with Christ, but now it was time, and I lacked the strength to carry the cross. I was defeated.

Then by the grace of God, the bar of the cross was taken for me. I was at the crucifixion site and I could see three crosses. I thought that I would be lifted onto a cross next to Jesus. Instead, for a moment the Spirit let me see things from an elevated, third person perspective. I looked down at the centre cross and saw Jesus. I could see through the cross and through Jesus. I was then taken back into my body and I was lifted up onto *His* cross. My hands went into His hands, my legs into his legs and my torso into His torso. My entire body was encompassed by Him.

I then felt death begin to come over me, starting at my feet. As I watched, my feet seemed to disappear entirely, consumed by the void of death. I was being reduced to nothing. My legs followed as death continued to devour me. In just a few seconds, it had reached my chest. All I could think was, "Is this it? Is this it? Is this it?" Finally, the question was answered. The darkness of death reached my head, and I was gone.

When death came to my eyes, I expected everything to go black. Instead, the opposite happened. I was surrounded by a blinding white light. Slowly my eyes adjusted and I could see. I was in the tomb, looking at the opening where the stone had been rolled away. I could barely believe what was happening.

I remained on my knees trying to take it all in. I had not spoken a word to anyone in the room during the vision. As I knelt there, looking at the doorway of the empty tomb, a friend in the group stepped forward, took me by the hand and lifted me up and declared: "Arise and shine! For your light has come and the glory of the Lord has risen upon you!"

I stood up and remembered that the Greek word for resurrection means "to stand up again." Had I been spiritually raised with Jesus? I stood there, too stunned to share the vision with anyone. I drove home that night and went to bed, still in shock. The next morning, I woke up to find the Holy Spirit moving over me in waves of life and energy, like spiritual plasma.

"This is different." I walked outside and realised exactly how different. The selfish nature was gone. The warfare of the heart was over. My enemy was defeated and in its place, I felt a deep and abiding peace. Every desire to sin was gone. I was free.

I felt born again, again. Like a new-born baby, I needed to learn life all over again. I did not feel proud, but neither did I feel humble. I felt neither greedy nor generous. I was a blank slate; a fresh field, ready to be planted with some good seed. God had kept His promise to circumcise my heart and now it was truly no longer I who lived, but Christ who lived in me. Now I could begin to live a life in design.

I smiled and praised God. It was a beautiful day.

Pray

Jesus, I want to experience the power of your death and the glory of your resurrection life. I choose life today. I invite you Holy Spirit to lead me to the cross and beyond! Please immerse me in the death of Christ and let me be raised to the newness of life. And may it all be to your great glory!

16 | Righteous Judgment

Luke 12:49-50 (BSB)
"I have come to ignite a fire on the earth, and how I wish it were already kindled! But I have a baptism to undergo, and how distressed I am until it is accomplished!"

One of the primary reasons Jesus came was to start a fire on the earth. Jesus wished that the fire was already kindled but He could not light it until He had been baptised. Jesus had already been baptised in water and in the Spirit, so what baptism was He yet to experience?

Mark 10:35-40
And James and John, the sons of Zebedee, came up to him and said to him, "Teacher, we want you to do for us whatever we ask of you." And he said to them, "What do you want me to do for you?" And they said to him, "Grant us to sit, one at your right hand and one at your left, in your glory." Jesus said to them, "You do not know what you are asking. Are you able to drink the cup that I drink, or to be baptised with the baptism with which I am baptised?" And they said to him, "We are able." And Jesus said to them, "The cup that I drink you will drink, and with the baptism with which I am baptised, you will be baptised, but to sit at my right hand or at my left is not mine to grant, but it is for those for whom it has been prepared."

"Are you able to drink the cup that I drink, or be baptised with the baptism with which I am baptised?" In this passage, Jesus connects drinking from the cup and being baptised. He invites His disciples to drink from His cup and

receive the same baptism. Do we have the courage to drink from His cup or be baptised with Him? What does it even mean to spiritually drink from the cup of Christ and be immersed with His baptism?

Cup of Wrath

Jeremiah 25:15

Thus the LORD, the God of Israel, said to me: "Take from my hand this cup of the wine of wrath, and make all the nations to whom I send you drink it."

In Scripture, the *cup* is often used as a metaphor for what people or nations receive from God. Most often it is used to speak of the anger or wrath of God.[1]

Romans 1:18

For the wrath of God is revealed from heaven against all ungodliness and unrighteousness of men, who by their unrighteousness suppress the truth.

People can sometimes struggle to believe that a God of absolute love can get angry. But His anger is a necessary quality of His love. In order to be perfect, love cannot tolerate evil forever. How could it? As parents, would we watch as a cancer kills our child when we could bring healing? Would not our love for our child cause us to hate the cancer and act to destroy it? It is the same for God. His love for us never wavers and He is *never* angry with us. Rather, His anger burns against all the ungodliness and unrighteousness within us.[2] He knows that the selfish nature is not us. He did not create it, nor did He design us to live with sin. Therefore, God's hatred towards the sinful nature burns with the same intensity as His love towards us. He loathes the sinful nature and if we let Him, He will destroy it.

John 3:36

"Whoever believes in [into] the Son has eternal life; whoever does not obey the Son shall not see life, but the wrath of God remains on him."

When we believe into Jesus, we come into union with Him. Our identity is no longer found in our old life but in the life we now share with Jesus. Those who do not follow Jesus live in unity with their flesh and their identity remains entwined with their selfish nature. God loves these people beyond all imagination and He calls us to share His love for them. He seeks them out, patiently waiting for people to come to repentance. But there will be a day when His love simply must consume all ungodliness. If people reject God and stubbornly remain one with their flesh, then they can expect to experience the wrath of God when it is released upon their selfish nature. This does not bear thinking about. Our mission is clear: Let us call everyone into their design of love while there is still time.

Drinking from the Cup

Luke 22:41-42
And he withdrew from them about a stone's throw, and knelt down and prayed, saying, "Father, if you are willing, remove this cup from me. Nevertheless, not my will, but yours, be done."

John 18:11
So Jesus said to Peter, "Put your sword into its sheath; shall I not drink the cup that the Father has given me?"

When Jesus prayed in the garden of Gethsemane, He asked God to remove the cup from Him. Jesus had only ever known the overwhelming love of God and so He had no desire to experience the Father's anger. Yet because of His love for us and His obedience to the Father, Jesus went to the cross, took the cup of God's wrath and utterly drained it.

2 Corinthians 5:20-21
Therefore, we are ambassadors for Christ, God making his appeal through us. We implore you on behalf of Christ, be reconciled to God. For our sake he made him to be sin who knew no sin, so that in him we might become the righteousness of God.

Romans 8:1-4
There is therefore now no condemnation for those who are in Christ Jesus. For the law of the Spirit of life has set you free in Christ Jesus from the law of sin and death. For God has done what the law, weakened by the flesh, could not do. By sending his own Son in the likeness of sinful flesh and for sin, he condemned sin in the flesh, in order that the righteous requirement of the law might be fulfilled in us, who walk not according to the flesh but according to the Spirit.

When Jesus went to the cross and drank the sour wine, He took on the likeness of sinful flesh and became sin. *Jesus became sin.* The extent of Christ's sacrifice was such that even the serpent, which typically represents evil, became a picture of Jesus at His death on the cross.[3]

These verses show the totality of God in dealing with sin. Nothing of Christ was held back—His whole being was given as a sacrifice so that sin could be utterly condemned in Him. This condemnation was a legal verdict which passed a death sentence upon the sin nature. Jesus then executed that judgment immediately. Having become sin, Jesus embraced death.

Through His sacrifice, the justice and mercy of God were both perfectly fulfilled. Complete justice was done as Christ suffered the highest penalty that the Law could give: death. This was not just the death of Jesus, but the death of all our sin in Him. Because justice was fully served at the cross, the mercy of God could be fully released to us. This mercy not only secured our forgiveness, but it assured our complete deliverance from the sin nature.

When we see the cross as the end of sin, we can see how the Father and Son so beautifully destroyed the works of the enemy. There was no sense of striving or human effort to bring about victory. There was only sacrificial love, and it was enough. Through love, Jesus submitted Himself to death on the cross. Through love, He took our sinful nature into hell and left it there. Through love, Jesus also passed judgment upon the ruler of this world. Without the sin nature ruling over people, Satan lost his authority on earth and fell, disarmed, humiliated, and condemned. He could then only watch on in defeat as Jesus rose again victorious over sin and death. It was finished.

Baptised in Fire

> Isaiah 66:15-16
>
> "For behold, the Lord will come in fire,
>   and his chariots like the whirlwind,
>   to render his anger in fury,
>   and his rebuke with flames of fire.
> For by fire will the Lord enter into judgment,
>   and by his sword, with all flesh;
>   and those slain by the Lord shall be many."

Scripture often uses fire as a symbol of the judgment of God.[4] It is a vivid picture of the intense wrath of God that consumes sin and evil. This fire of judgment connects Christ's cup and His baptism. At the cross, Jesus became sin. He then drank the cup of God's wrath and allowed the judgment of God to totally immerse Him. This was His baptism of fire and every part of Him burned. There is now no longer any sacrifice required for sin because in Jesus Christ, sin itself has been completely consumed.

> 1 Corinthians 11:31-32
>
> But if we judged ourselves truly, we would not be judged. But when we are judged by the Lord, we are disciplined so that we may not be condemned along with the world.

It is a part of every believer's inheritance to experience the glory of God's judgment upon our sin nature *in this life*. This is a gift of extreme grace to us. No one deserves to be free from the sinful nature, for we all chose to embrace it. But in His grace, God judges and condemns it, crucifies it, removes it, and sets us free to be one with Christ.

This is an awesome picture of the love of God in action. As an act of love, God's judgment is not something that we should fear but rather something to long for. So let us surrender our flesh to the cross! Let us give our loving Father permission to be our righteous Judge! May He then bring us into the freedom and glory He designed for us. Faithful is He who calls us. He can do it. And He will.

Pray

Holy Spirit, I invite you to take me into the reality of God's judgment. I want my flesh to be judged, condemned, and completely consumed. I ask you to release the full power of the cross in my life.

17 | Immersed in Fire

Matthew 3:10-12

"Even now the axe is laid to the root of the trees. Every tree therefore that does not bear good fruit is cut down and thrown into the fire.

"I baptise you with water for repentance, but he who is coming after me is mightier than I, whose sandals I am not worthy to carry. He will baptise you with the Holy Spirit and fire. His winnowing fork is in his hand, and he will clear his threshing floor and gather his wheat into the barn, but the chaff he will burn with unquenchable fire."

Here John the Baptist says that Jesus is coming to baptise people with the Holy Spirit and fire. Jesus will separate the wheat from the chaff; the wheat will be gathered to Him and the chaff will be consumed in unquenchable fire.

In this passage, John talks about judgment as a present reality rather than a future event at the end of time. He also speaks of the baptism of fire as a spiritual experience that we can have as individuals. How can we be sure? Because it is a baptism. Just as each one of us is individually baptised in water and in the Spirit, so we all need to personally experience the baptism of fire.

Later in the book of Matthew, Jesus speaks of the wheat and the weeds (tares) in a corporate way, revealing an inescapable, end-time judgment. So there is a judgment that *anyone* can experience now by faith, and a future judgment that *everyone* will experience apart from faith. It is real, and it will happen. But as this passage makes clear: we do not need to wait until the end of time to experience the blessing of God's judgment. If we are willing, Jesus will baptise us with His fire in this life.

Matthew 13:24-30

He put another parable before them, saying, "The kingdom of heaven may be compared to a man who sowed good seed in his field, but while his men were sleeping, his enemy came and sowed weeds among the wheat and went away. So when the plants came up and bore grain, then the weeds appeared also. And the servants of the master of the house came and said to him, 'Master, did you not sow good seed in your field? How then does it have weeds?' He said to them, 'An enemy has done this.' So the servants said to him, 'Then do you want us to go and gather them?' But he said, 'No, lest in gathering the weeds you root up the wheat along with them. Let both grow together until the harvest, and at harvest time I will tell the reapers, "Gather the weeds first and bind them in bundles to be burned, but gather the wheat into my barn."'"

In this parable, the weeds were only burned after they were separated from the wheat. As we learned earlier, in our spiritual infancy, we have little ability to separate the selfish nature of the flesh from our true nature. Yet as we grow, we begin to forge our true identity in unity with Jesus. We learn about who we really are in Christ and who we are not. We learn to no longer see ourselves as sinful, selfish, proud, greedy, lustful, fearful, violent, insecure or unloving. On the contrary, in Christ we are loving, selfless, generous, hopeful, positive, compassionate, optimistic, and spiritually beautiful. As we turn against our selfish nature and break all agreements with it, the weeds are separated from the wheat and, we can then experience the baptism of fire. God immerses us in His judgment and consumes our flesh, burning away the root of sin within us and destroying every instinct and desire to sin. Then we are truly free to love God with all our heart and soul.

One Baptism

Ephesians 4:4-6

There is one body and one Spirit—just as you were called to the one hope that belongs to your call—one Lord, one faith, one baptism, one God and Father of all, who is over all and through all and in all.

Scripture speaks of one baptism into Christ. Yet it also speaks of being baptised in water, spirit and in fire.

The baptism in water is a baptism of repentance for the forgiveness of sins.[1] It is a physical act that represents leaving our old life and starting a new life with God.

The **baptism in the Spirit** is an immersion into the Spirit of Jesus—a complete saturation in His life, presence, and power. It is an ongoing spiritual experience that brings us into ever deepening unity with Jesus.

The **baptism in fire** is an immersion in the judgment of God. God's wrath falls upon our selfish nature and it is then consumed by the fire of God. This baptism unites us with Christ in His death.

> **John 16:7-11**
> "Nevertheless, I tell you the truth: it is to your advantage that I go away, for if I do not go away, the Helper will not come to you. But if I go, I will send him to you. And when he comes, he will convict the world concerning sin and righteousness and judgment: concerning sin, because they do not believe in me; concerning righteousness, because I go to the Father, and you will see me no longer; concerning judgment, because the ruler of this world is judged."

The Father sent the Holy Spirit to convict the world of sin, righteousness, and judgment. Through the conviction of sin, the Spirit leads a person to the baptism in water for repentance and the forgiveness of sins. Through the conviction of righteousness, the Spirit leads a person to the baptism in the Spirit so they can share the righteousness of Christ.[2] Lastly, by the conviction of judgment, the Spirit leads a person into the baptism of fire to destroy their sin nature.

Fire of Love

> **1 John 4:9-10** (NLT)
> God showed how much he loved us by sending his one and only Son into the world so that we might have eternal life through him. This is

real love—not that we loved God, but that he loved us and sent his Son as a sacrifice to take away our sins.

The cross was the ultimate place of judgment, justice and mercy. But most of all, it was the ultimate place of love. The Father showed the full extent of His love by sending His Son to die. Jesus, the King of Glory, humbled Himself by allowing His creation to torture Him, humiliate Him, and kill Him. Jesus was so determined to see our design of love restored that He gladly embraced the cross. His motive was love, His means were love, and His goal was love.

Song of Solomon 8:6
"Set me as a seal upon your heart,
    as a seal upon your arm,
for love is strong as death,
    jealousy is fierce as the grave.
Its flashes are flashes of fire,
    the very flame of the LORD."

Here Scripture likens love to fire—the very flame of the LORD. It can be tempting to separate the judgment of God from His love. But God does not suspend His love while He releases His judgment, not even for a moment. In fact, it is the opposite. The fire we call God's judgment is the fire of His love.

When God pours out the fire of His love, it engulfs everything it touches. Yet like gold, that which is of God survives the fire while everything else burns. This makes the baptism of fire a place of ultimate safety for us.

We can see the power of God's fire in the story of Daniel's friends who were thrown into the fiery furnace.[3] In the fire they encountered Jesus and when they came out of the fire they were unharmed in any way—only their bonds were burned away. It is the same for us. When we enter the baptism of fire, we encounter Jesus as the Refiner's Fire. His love consumes our bondage of sin and selfishness. After it has done its refining, we emerge from the fire energised and unharmed, sharing a new depth of unity with Jesus.

An Ongoing Immersion

In *First Love,* we learned that baptism is not just a one-off experience but an ongoing immersion. For example, the baptism of the Spirit does not end when we are first filled with the Spirit, but it continues as we are filled over and over again. The same is true for the baptism of fire. When we are first immersed in the fire of God, Jesus burns away our sin and completely purifies our hearts. Yet our immersion in fire does not stop there. God is a consuming fire of love. After our flesh nature is destroyed, the love of Christ continues to burn within us. And there is simply no limit to how brightly His fire can burn.

God's nature of perfect love demands that He always seeks the very best for us. Even though we do not deserve it, God must seek our best in order to remain true to Himself. And what is best? God's best vision for our life is one of unfailing love, intense intimacy, and extreme unity with Him. This was always His design, but it has been constantly sabotaged by the selfish nature within us. In order to overcome the sin nature, the Father sent Jesus to deal with it once and for all.

When Jesus came to earth, His passion was to release the baptism of fire so people could be consumed with His love. In the last chapter, we saw how this passion left Him in a place of deep distress. Jesus wished the fire of His love could be poured out upon His people, but He knew that He had to first be baptised in fire on our behalf so our sin could be consumed.

Even now, Jesus is still distressed. He longs to release the full force of the cross in our lives, but He must wait for our permission. The cross now stands waiting as our altar. Our call is to offer ourselves as living sacrifices upon the altar and wait for His fire to fall. And like Elijah at Mount Carmel, we can be absolutely certain it will happen. If we fully surrender our lives to Him, Jesus Himself will baptise us in the fire of His love. He died for this and right now He is distressed until He can make it a reality in our lives. Let us end His distress. Let us embrace the cross and enter the fire. He is waiting.

Pray

Jesus, thank you for making a way for me to be baptised in your fire. Let your love consume every part of my being. Let it destroy everything in me that is not of you. Then let the fire of your love blaze within me. When people look me in the eyes, may they see your fire burning brightly.

18 | Judgment and Design

I have a friend who once took a group of young people into a gym for a game. He threw a ball into the middle of the court and yelled "Go! Get the ball in the goal!" Everyone ran to get the ball and fought to take control of it so they could score a goal. But there was no goal. At times, the young people were confused, but they were quickly distracted by the competition over the ball. For the most part, the goal was barely given any thought. Everyone was having fun playing a chaotic, confusing, and ultimately futile game.

For so many people, this is a picture of our spiritual life. We are so zealous for God and so busy in activity for Him, that we forget to consider the goal. We simply do not think to ask God what we are called to do and why. Yet there will come a day when our time runs out and it will be game over.

Eternal Judgment

> Hebrews 6:1-3 (BSB)
> Therefore let us leave the elementary teachings about Christ and go on to maturity, not laying again the foundation of repentance from dead works, and of faith in God, instruction about baptisms, the laying on of hands, the resurrection of the dead, and eternal judgment. And this we will do, if God permits.

No competitive athlete would enter a competition without knowing where the finish line is and how to win. Likewise, a good student will always know what they will be tested on and prepare in advance. In the same way, eternal judgment is one of the elementary teachings that we all must learn because it defines our goal. Once we know where our goal is, we are empowered with a direction for our life. We can then make decisions and take actions that make sense according to our future judgment. Jesus often speaks of the Day of Judgment for exactly this reason, so we can clearly understand the goal of life. Judgment is real, it is coming, and we need to get ready.

The best way to prepare for judgment is to understand what we will be judged on. Earlier we looked at the metaphor of being a clockmaker. If we made a clock and had to give it one single command, we would simply say: *tell the time.* That one command would communicate the whole purpose of the clock. Now, if we were to judge our clock, we would judge it solely on its ability to tell the time accurately.[1]

In every sphere of life, judgment is always connected to design and it will be the same for us on the final Day of Judgment. We only have a short time to prepare, and so we need to fully invest our lives in God's design of love.

Design of Love

> **Matthew 22:35-40**
>
> And one of them, a lawyer, asked him a question to test him. "Teacher, which is the great commandment in the Law?" And he said to him, "You shall love the Lord your God with all your heart and with all your soul and with all your mind. This is the great and first commandment. And a second is like it: You shall love your neighbour as yourself. On these two commandments depend all the Law and the Prophets."

There are two levels of design in life: our design as individuals in relationship with God, and our corporate design in relationship with each other. The first and greatest command speaks of our design as individuals: Each one of us has been wonderfully made and perfectly designed to love God with our entire being. The second command speaks of our design corporately: As channels of God's love, we are called to let His love flow through us to the people around us.

A New Command

John 13:34-35
A new commandment I give to you, that you love one another: just as I have loved you, you also are to love one another. By this all people will know that you are my disciples, if you have love for one another."

In this passage, Jesus gives us one new command: to love one another. But does this mean that the first and greatest command is no longer first? Has Jesus now elevated our love for people above our love for God?

Colossians 1:27
To them God chose to make known how great among the Gentiles are the riches of the glory of this mystery, which is Christ in you, the hope of glory.

One of the greatest mysteries of faith is that Jesus Christ dwells within His people. This truth is foundational to our whole understanding of the gospel and of the purpose of God for our lives. We are only made righteous because the Spirit of Jesus lives within us and shares His righteousness with us. We are only made holy because Jesus lives within us and shares His holiness with us. We only experience the fruit of the Spirit because we have the Holy Spirit *within us*. Our entire life flows from the unity that we share with the Spirit of God. We are one with Him.

The new command is set entirely in the context of our unity with Jesus. By giving us one new command, Jesus is not diminishing the first command in any way. Instead, He is combining the first and second commands of love into one new command and showing us that because He lives within us, **we love Him by loving one another.**

1 John 4:7-11
Beloved, let us love one another, for love is from God, and whoever loves has been born of God and knows God. Anyone who does not love does not know God, because God is love. In this the love of God was made manifest among us, that God sent his only Son into the world,

so that we might live through him. In this is love, not that we have loved God but that he loved us and sent his Son to be the propitiation for our sins. Beloved, if God so loved us, we also ought to love one another. No one has ever seen God; if we love one another, God abides in us and his love is perfected in us.

In our modern Christian culture, many people assume that we love Jesus by singing songs to Him. Jesus delights in our praise for sure, but while our songs convey our sincere affection for Him, they rarely express selfless, sacrificial love. In terms of loving Jesus, we need to add actions to our words.

When we share the Father's love for Jesus, it will naturally flow to Jesus where He is living: in His people. This is why Scripture says that if we love one another, we abide in God and His love is perfected in us. The Father's love is made perfect in us only as it actively flows to His Son in the people around us. When we see our relationships as channels of love between the Father and the Son, we will be confident in God's unlimited provision for love. The Father will always give us whatever we need to love His Son through His people. How could He not?

The worldwide Church so desperately needs this truth of "Christ in us" to become her revelation and reality. While most Christians would say they believe that Jesus lives within His people, few act as though it were true. Imagine if we could look at a person and see through them to Jesus. Imagine listening to someone speak and hearing the voice of Christ. Imagine seeing the heart of God revealed in His people. Imagine looking into someone's eyes and seeing the fire of Christ's love burning in them! The only reason we do not see Jesus in His people is that we do not look for Him. If we truly believed that the Spirit of Jesus dwells in His people, we would actively seek out each other's needs and do whatever we could to meet them. We would listen to one another, invest time in each other, encourage one another, forgive one other, seek each other's best, and lavish one another with honour, grace, and love. This is God's perfect design for life, and it is glorious beyond words.

Judgment and Design

Matthew 25:31-40

"When the Son of Man comes in his glory, and all the angels with him, then he will sit on his glorious throne. Before him will be gathered all the nations, and he will separate people one from another as a shepherd separates the sheep from the goats. And he will place the sheep on his right, but the goats on the left. Then the King will say to those on his right, 'Come, you who are blessed by my Father, inherit the kingdom prepared for you from the foundation of the world. For I was hungry and you gave me food, I was thirsty and you gave me drink, I was a stranger and you welcomed me, I was naked and you clothed me, I was sick and you visited me, I was in prison and you came to me.' Then the righteous will answer him, saying, 'Lord, when did we see you hungry and feed you, or thirsty and give you drink? And when did we see you a stranger and welcome you, or naked and clothe you? And when did we see you sick or in prison and visit you?' And the King will answer them, 'Truly, I say to you, as you did it to one of the least of these my brothers, you did it to me.'"

When we give ourselves to be a temple for the Spirit of Jesus, we invite Jesus to share His life with us, and we likewise share our life with Him. This means that through His Spirit, Jesus shares our experiences and He shares our need. Imagine it: The infinite God who needs nothing, humbles Himself to share all our pain, all our lack, all our weakness, and all our need. And He does it all for love.

So when we ease someone's pain, we give comfort to Jesus who is sharing that pain with that person. When we bless someone, we bless Jesus, who is living in that person. And when we give to meet a person's need, we love Jesus by meeting His need. It is essential that we truly understand this. The Spirit of Jesus dwells in His people and so the primary way we love Jesus is by meeting the needs of His people.

> 1 John 3:23
> And this is his commandment, that we believe in the name of his Son Jesus Christ and love one another, just as he has commanded us.

It is almost certain that many of the goats will have believed they were sheep. Many will have attended church their entire lives, thinking that the eternal judgment is a matter of intellectual belief rather than love in action. Yet here John makes it clear: The Father gives us one command which is to believe in Jesus *and* love one another. There is no separation between faith and love; in fact, true faith will always express itself through sacrificial love. Therefore, when Jesus takes all humanity into the eternal judgment, He will open the book of life, containing all the names of those people who chose life in Christ and lived in love, intimacy and unity with Him. He will then judge our faith not on what we said we believed in this life, but on how we have expressed our faith by loving Him through His people.

Confidence in the Day of Judgment

> 1 John 4:14b-21
> So we have come to know and to believe the love that God has for us. God is love, and whoever abides in love abides in God, and God abides in him. By this is love perfected with us, so that we may have confidence for the day of judgment, because as he is so also are we in this world. There is no fear in love, but perfect love casts out fear. For fear has to do with punishment, and whoever fears has not been perfected in love. We love because he first loved us. If anyone says, "I love God," and hates his brother, he is a liar; for he who does not love his brother whom he has seen cannot love God whom he has not seen. And this commandment we have from him: whoever loves God must also love his brother.

God does not intend for our eternal judgment to be uncertain or mysterious in any way. As a good teacher, God has already given us both the questions and the answers to our final exam. Even more than that—He has sat the exam and passed, and now He wants to pass for us! All we need to do is be crucified with Christ and let Jesus live His life of love through us.

When we live as channels of the Father's love for Jesus, we can have confidence for the day of final judgment, because we know exactly what we will be judged upon. *Did we love Jesus through His people? Did we meet His needs that He shared with people? Did we express the Father's love for Jesus in our relationships with other believers? Yes! Yes! Yes! It was our vision, our goal, and our delight!*

It is this flow of perfect love through us that casts out all fear of judgment. We know we are His sheep because we are living in God's design. The Father is filling us with His love for Jesus and we are letting that love flow to Christ by speaking words of love to one another and meeting each other's needs. Our love for one another is therefore the proof that we have passed from death to life.[2] Jesus has saved us from the death of our selfishness and brought us into a life of love, intimacy and unity with Him. To God be the glory!

Pray

Father, I thank you for your awesome design of love. Thank you that it is so simple. You created me to be a channel of your love for Jesus. Please open my eyes to see Jesus in His people and open my heart for your love to flow. I give everything I am and everything I have to loving Jesus. Let your love flow!

PART THREE | FIGHT FOR LIFE

19 | Renewing the Mind

Being crucified with Christ is not the end of our journey, but a new beginning. After we experience the removal of the old self, we will have a sense of profound, abiding peace, and we will be free from the innate desire to sin. But this does not equate to instant, perfect Christlikeness. Becoming one with Christ is a journey into the infinite love of God. And it is a journey we take together with other believers as we love one another.

There will always be times along this journey when we need to face and overcome the enemy. Victory over the selfish nature is only one of several battlegrounds. Areas of our overcoming and transformation include:

1. The heart—removing the selfish nature, partaking of the nature of Christ, and being filled with God's love
2. The mind—renewing our old mindsets and learning to share the mind of Christ
3. The body—cleansing our inherited genetic profile
4. The spirit—overcoming demonic spirits and being possessed by the Spirit of Jesus

In the next few chapters, we will look at overcoming in the realm of the body and spirit, however, for now we will focus on the mind and explore some of the ways the Holy Spirit renews our mind. A key part of this renewing is learning how to live in unity with Jesus. What does it look like to live every moment with Him? How does His constant presence within us change the way we think?

An Ongoing Renewing

> **Romans 12:1-2** (TDB)
> I appeal to you therefore, brothers, by the mercies of God, to present✓ your bodies as a living sacrifice, holy and acceptable to God, which is your spiritual worship. Do not be conformed~ to this world, but be transformed~ by the renewal of your mind, that by testing you may discern~ what is the will of God, what is good and acceptable and perfect.

In this passage, we find the Greek aorist (✓) and present tense (~).[1] The aorist speaks of a one-off action at a point in time. In contrast, the Greek present tense speaks of an ongoing, continual, or habitual action.

Paul calls us to offer our bodies as a one-off living sacrifice (aorist), and then be continually transformed by the renewing of our minds (present tense). This offering of our bodies is like the one-off decision we make to follow Jesus. It is a decision that happens at a point in time, but one that has daily consequences that we will feel for the rest of our lives.

In the same way, being crucified with Christ is a one-off experience that has lifelong consequences. However, just like our initial decision to follow Jesus, there can be a process involved in coming to this point of truly offering ourselves to God and being crucified with Christ. But if we keep leaning on God, He will help us to lay our lives on the altar of the cross. Then the fire will fall and it will change everything. We will feel a deep peace and the end of conflict within our souls. We will no longer feel any instinct or desire to sin. And because this comes as a real spiritual experience, we will have a testimony that we can share with others.

> **Ephesians 4:20-24** (TDB)
> But that is not the way you learned Christ!— assuming that you have heard about him and were taught in him, as the truth is in Jesus, to put off✓ your old self, which belongs to your former manner of life and is corrupt through deceitful desires, and to be renewed~ in the spirit of your minds, and to put on✓ the new self, created after the likeness of God in true righteousness and holiness.

This passage echoes Romans 12. Here Scripture calls us to completely put off the old self and put on the new self. In terms of the removal of the selfish nature, here again the Greek aorist describes this as a one-off experience that happens at a point in time. And again the present tense is used to call us to continually renew in our minds.

The picture that Scripture paints is that after we have been crucified with Christ, we still need to keep on renewing our minds. The sinful nature has had years to warp the way we think, and this damage needs to be undone.

It is often quoted that the Greek word *metanoia*, which is translated as *repentance*, means to change the mind. But true repentance reaches beyond the intellect and requires us to change what we know at a heart level. It calls us to reject any unity with our flesh nature. Instead, we are to turn to the Lord and come to know Him through love, intimacy and unity with Jesus.

Repentance therefore deals with both the heart and the mind. Our hearts receive a transplant as Jesus replaces our selfish nature with His nature of love, and our minds are changed through a process of renewing.

This renewing is outworked in relationship with God rather than something we try to do on our own. Our part is to invite the Holy Spirit to speak to us about areas of our thinking that are not aligned with His truth. When He does this, we give these areas to Him and invite the Spirit to replace them with His thoughts. The same is true for renewing our feelings. It is all about an ongoing process of change and exchange that comes from relating with Jesus. The more we let Him renew our thoughts and feelings, the more transformed we become.

Tearing Down Strongholds

2 Corinthians 10:4-5
For the weapons of our warfare are not of the flesh but have divine power to destroy strongholds. We destroy arguments and every lofty opinion raised against the knowledge of God, and take every thought captive to obey Christ...

At times the renewing of the mind can be quick and effortless as the Holy Spirit gives us new insights and reveals new truth. At other times it can be like laying siege to a stronghold. In *First Love,* we looked at how strongholds are mindsets or biases that shape the way we interpret life and how we view God. Often these strongholds are built upon established patterns of thinking that have real power to affect our feelings and our behaviour.

Our goal is to build godly strongholds. These are mindsets that are formed by faith and built upon the truth. At the same time, we also need to deal with ungodly strongholds of the mind. Ungodly strongholds have been created by the flesh and are founded upon lies. Therefore, after the flesh nature has been removed from our hearts, we need to destroy any remaining strongholds by dealing with the lies they are built on.

It is the Holy Spirit's work to renew our mind and we need to trust Him to lead us in it. If the Spirit confronts a stronghold, ask Him to reveal the lies that are at its foundation. For example, a stronghold of fear may be built upon a lie that was first believed as a child, *I cannot trust anyone to keep me safe, not even God*. Once the lie is exposed, we can take the following steps to deal with it.

1. Repent from believing the lie
2. Forgive anyone that the Lord brings to mind
3. Release anyone from any judgments or curses that you made against them as you built these strongholds
4. Ask God to give you His truth in exchange for the lie
5. Meditate on the truth He reveals to you and give the Holy Spirit space to impress it onto your heart and soul[2]

Strongholds and the Flesh

It is important to discern the difference between the negative strongholds of the mind and the flesh nature. Strongholds are false beliefs that exist in the mind and corrupt the way we think. The flesh nature is a cancer that takes root in the heart and creates our selfish instincts. Because the flesh nature is not a part of our design, Scripture's only solution is to crucify it. We cannot cast it out. It cannot be healed or redeemed, and it certainly cannot be renewed. Without the cross, there is no way we can overcome the flesh. It simply must die.

Unlike the flesh nature, our mind is a part of God's design. Therefore we cannot cast it out, nor can we kill it or remove it. The only way we can deal with the negative strongholds of the mind is by letting Jesus share His thoughts with us and change the way we think. The more we hear His voice and consume His word, the more our minds are renewed.

If we fail to recognise the difference between the mind and the flesh, we risk ending up in a place of spiritual confusion. We saw this confusion earlier, where we looked at the teaching that says the flesh nature is killed when we first believe. In order to explain why believers still have sinful instincts after conversion, this teaching says that the instinct to sin does not come from a person's selfish nature, but from their belief in a lie. Because they think that sin is driven by a false belief, they teach that the way to overcome sin is by renewing the mind.

There is always fruit in renewing the mind, but without the circumcision of the heart, the renewing of the mind will *never* bring anyone full freedom. To think that we can renew our way out of our sinful instincts is like believing we can talk ourselves out of addiction. The problem is in the nature of the heart not the thinking of the mind! To be clear, the renewing of the mind is essential for every believer. It is part of a living relationship with Jesus. But it will *never* replace the circumcision of the heart.

Inner-Healing Therapy

Those who ignore the ongoing impact of the flesh nature or deny its presence within a believer often trap people in an unending therapy culture. They create an expectation that we will always struggle with sin for the rest of our lives but insist that it will get easier the more we renew our mind. People accept the struggle and naturally think, *"When God heals me of my trauma, then I will be effective in the Kingdom. When God restores my marriage, I'll impact the world for Him. I cannot love others because I am not truly loving myself. I am just too broken to be useful to God. When He heals me, then I'll devote my life to Him."* When people think like this, they make an idol of their brokenness and effectively blame their lack of obedience on God due to His lack of healing. This kind of attitude is created by the flesh to ensure its own survival. It puts the focus on a person's brokenness and robs them of any faith or vision for a life of love.

People genuinely want to be free from their selfish nature, and so they seek healing or teaching to find wholeness. They view their recovery as a long process that requires a constant flow of teaching, ministry, counselling, prayer or even sermons. But this all misses the point. No amount of teaching can remove the flesh nature. No amount of ministry or counselling can kill it. The only way to deal with the flesh is to crucify it with Christ—not in theory but in actual, spiritual experience. Only once the flesh nature is removed can inner-healing truly begin.[3]

Before all this can happen, people must first devote their lives to loving God with all their heart and soul. This devotion activates His promise to make it a reality. His design is one of *whole*-hearted love, which means that if we are truly willing, God must not only remove the flesh nature, but He must also heal every last wound of the heart and make it completely whole.

God's greatest command is His greatest promise, and it must become both the starting point and the goal of all our ministry. Think: if we were ministering to broken clocks, our focus would always be to help them tell the time. In the same way, all our teaching, counselling, prophecy, evangelism and discipleship must direct people through the cross to their design of love. This is the only way to complete freedom, healing and wholeness. After God has brought them into the circumcision of the heart, we can then focus on renewing the mind.

No Longer I

Galatians 2:20

I have been crucified with Christ. It is no longer I who live, but Christ who lives in me. And the life I now live in the flesh I live by faith in the Son of God, who loved me and gave himself for me.

This verse contains one of the most powerful keys to renewing the mind. When we are crucified with Christ, we begin life again in unity with Jesus and need to account for our unity with Jesus in the way we think. In *First Love*, we learn how we can do this simply by taking captive any *I* thoughts and change them to *We*.

"I'm not enough" becomes "We are enough."

"I can't do this" becomes "We can do this."

"I don't want to..." becomes "Do we want to..?"

Thinking *We* invites Jesus into our thinking and forces us to accept the truth that Jesus is living in us and we are one with Him. To be clear: thinking *We* does not mean thinking that we are God. God alone is God and He is not us. But we cannot deny the truth that Jesus lives within us. We are temples of His Spirit and channels of His love. We therefore need to learn how to renew our minds and start thinking in terms of the unity we have with Him. This can all start now. Let us change "*I* could never think this way" to "*We...*"

Pray

Jesus, I love you! Thank you that you want to share your mind with me. Please help me to become sensitive to your thoughts. Holy Spirit, please show me areas of my thinking that are not aligned with your truth. Renew me today so that I can grow in my love for Jesus and in thinking We!

20 | Blessing or Curse?

Deuteronomy 30:19-20
"I call heaven and earth to witness against you today, that I have set before you life and death, blessing and curse. Therefore choose life, that you and your offspring may live, loving the Lord your God, obeying his voice and holding fast to him, for he is your life and length of days, that you may dwell in the land that the Lord swore to your fathers, to Abraham, to Isaac, and to Jacob, to give them."

The whole Bible speaks at length about blessings and curses. If we read it through the lens of legalism, we might see blessings as the reward of our righteous behaviour and curses as God's punishment for our bad behaviour. However, in this passage, blessing and curse are not based on behaviour but on a choice of faith. If we choose life by loving God, hearing His voice, and living in unity with Him, it will always bring forth blessing. Conversely, if we choose to live according to our selfish nature, we will experience the curse of spiritual desolation and death.[1]

Galatians 6:7-8
Do not be deceived: God is not mocked, for whatever one sows, that will he also reap. For the one who sows to his own flesh will from the flesh reap corruption, but the one who sows to the Spirit will from the Spirit reap eternal life.

Blessing and curses follow the law of reaping and sowing. No one thinks that God is punishing them when they plant a sour apple tree and then find that it bears sour apples. So why would we think that God is punishing us if we choose to act according to our selfish nature and then experience loss, pain or difficulty? God is not holding out blessing and curses as rewards or punishments to try and motivate us to act in a certain way. On the contrary, they are simply the fruit of a life rooted in the Spirit or rooted in the flesh.

The curses that God warns His people about only came because people did not follow Him "with joy and gladness of heart, for the abundance of everything."[2] In His infinite love, God wanted His people to experience a life of incredible joy and abundance. But the people were determined to go their own way. Though it took a few generations, once Israel had settled in the land and had all their physical needs met, they slowly rejected love, joy, intimacy and unity with their God. They chose to follow their own selfish pursuits and pleasures; they worshipped other gods and so chose death instead of life and curse instead of blessing.

This curse affected their whole lives. It led to the desolation of the land, their relationships, their work, their families, and even their entire nation. In our limited understanding, we think that we exist in isolation and that our choices only really affect us. But it is not true. God has woven His creation together so that what we do has rippling effects throughout the wider world. For this reason, when God blessed Abraham, He said that all the nations of the world will be blessed in him. It is the same for us. When we live a life of love and blessing, it will flow through to the world around us, impacting our families, our communities, our work, the land, and all our relationships.

When we live in selfless love, genuine blessing is hard to contain. It is something we want to share with the world. However, those who live according to the flesh also feel compelled to share their curse with others. Their choice for death not only affects them, but the world around them. In Psalm 109 David writes of such a man.

> **Psalm 109:14-20**
> Let the iniquity of his fathers be remembered before the Lord,
> And do not let the sin of his mother be blotted out.
> Let them be before the Lord continually,
> That He may cut off their memory from the earth;

> Because he did not remember to show lovingkindness,
> But persecuted the afflicted and needy man,
> And the despondent in heart, to put them to death.
> He also loved cursing, so it came to him;
> And he did not delight in blessing, so it was far from him.
> But he clothed himself with cursing as with his garment,
> And it entered into his body like water,
> And like oil into his bones.
> Let it be to him as a garment with which he covers himself,
> And for a belt with which he constantly girds himself.
> Let this be the reward of my accusers from the Lord,
> And of those who speak evil against my soul.

In this Psalm, David is speaking about a man who is living fully according to his selfish nature. He lies and spreads death wherever he goes. He does not show any love to anyone, nor does he delight in blessing. Instead, he loves cursing. He clothes himself with it and it enters his body like water and like oil in his bones. It is almost as if his whole being is changed by the curse that came when he rejected his design of love.

It is likely that the man in Psalm 109 did not consider himself to be particularly evil. Scripture even speaks of people who are so deceived that they call good evil and evil good.[3] Like such people, if we are not quick to repent, the deceitfulness of sin may lead us to justify our sin as normal behaviour. For example, there are many people who would rather justify their unforgiveness than repent. They do not see it as evil, and in fact many embrace it is as a healthy response to injustice. At this point, sin becomes iniquity—a sinful behaviour that is not thought of as sinful—and it begins to soak into our inner being and shape our identity. This iniquity then brings a curse that can affect generations to come.

Exodus 20:4-6
"You shall not make for yourself a carved image, or any likeness of anything that is in heaven above, or that is in the earth beneath, or that is in the water under the earth. You shall not bow down to them

or serve them, for I the Lord your God am a jealous God, visiting the iniquity of the fathers on the children to the third and the fourth generation of those who hate me, but showing steadfast love to thousands of those who love me and keep my commandments."

In this passage, we see how an agreement with a particular sin can be passed on to the next generation. But has not God already cancelled the curse? Are we not free from the previous generations and now only accountable for our own sin?

Science may help to answer this question. In 2013, scientists published the results of an experiment in which a trauma shaped the instinctive behaviour of three generations of mice.[4] In this experiment, a mouse was exposed to the smell of cherry blossom and given a light electric shock to his feet. This was done regularly over three days. That mouse then mated with a female. Not only were the offspring afraid of the smell of cherry blossom, but they could smell it at much lower levels than any of the other non-related mice. The fear experience of the father mouse had been passed onto the offspring through the tuning of their DNA.[5] And when the next generation of mice mated, their offspring also inherited the same instinct. Through no fault of their own, they had inherited the fear of cherry blossom.

Scientists call this field of study *epigenetics*, and it is a new field of study with much to discover. However, in these early stages of understanding, it appears that epigenetics may be one way that both blessings and curses are passed on from one generation to the next.

The point here is not that God punishes four generations for the sin of a single person, but that the following generations inherit both righteous or sinful inclinations (blessings or curses) based on the choices that an ancestor has made. If this dynamic is passed on to four generations, it means that we have a biological and spiritual profile that has been shaped by the life-experiences of 30 different people.[6]

Confess and Cleanse

We can often see these generational blessings and curses by looking at the patterns of behaviour that trace down the generations of our family. When I examined my life and the lives of my extended family and ancestors, I filled a page with different sins and curses. The Holy Spirit also prompted me to include some sins that I was not aware of in my generations. Most curses were broken with a single prayer, however, there were some like legalism and freemasonry which had deep roots that required more attention.

Though I felt nothing at the time when breaking the curses that had come from freemasonry, profound change quickly followed. It was like I had been living under a cloud and now the skies were clear. Dealing with generational curses costs us nothing but a few minutes of prayer and has the power to bring us into a significantly greater level of freedom and joy.

> **Leviticus 26:40-42**
> "But if they confess their iniquity and the iniquity of their fathers in their treachery that they committed against me, and also in walking contrary to me, so that I walked contrary to them and brought them into the land of their enemies—if then their uncircumcised heart is humbled and they make amends for their iniquity, then I will remember my covenant with Jacob, and I will remember my covenant with Isaac and my covenant with Abraham, and I will remember the land."

When I first heard about confessing the sins of our forefathers, I thought it made no sense. Surely we are only accountable for our own sin. While it is true that we are not condemned by another person's sin, the reality is that we carry within us the biological effects of our ancestors' sins. When we confess their sins, repent, and let the blood of Jesus cleanse us, our whole being is purified and the curse is broken. Even the expression of our DNA is restored. Having confessed our sin, we can then ask the Holy Spirit if there are any areas that we need to make amends.

Indolence

In the early years of my marriage and family, I was self-employed in software design. I spent a lot of time coding for people, but although I knew God had provided the work, a part of me did not want to do it. It did not seem to have any value compared to ministry and writing the *One with Christ* books. So I would often delay coding to invest time in more valuable pursuits.

One day, I was praying instead of working. As I prayed, I felt God say, "You need to repent from indolence."

I had no idea what the word *indolence* meant. I looked it up and found that indolence is "an aversion to work; avoidance of activity or exertion; laziness." Oh. God was showing what was really happening: I was using prayer as an excuse to justify not working. It was a form of procrastination for me that was sabotaging God's plans for my work. Worse still was that I was actively agreeing with a spirit of laziness, which distracted me from my work and made it a battle to get work done. *This work isn't spiritual. It has no eternal value. Don't waste your time.* The reality is that Jesus spent a lot of time as a carpenter and He was doing what the Father was doing the whole time. If God is in our work, it is a privilege to do it with Him.

I repented, "Father, I repent from indolence. I renounce it and reject it from my life. I break every agreement with laziness and procrastination. I cancel any legal right of the enemy to attack me in this area, and I expel any demonic spirit of laziness from my life. Jesus, I thank you for your blood that washes away all sin and completely cleanses me."

Some years later, my mother discussed some of our ancestry with me. On both sides, there were people who were known for their exceptional laziness. Indolence was running through the bloodline of my family. As I confessed and repented from laziness, the blood of Jesus cleansed my bloodline. Having removed the curse, I was then free to experience more of His energising grace. For as the Scriptures say: The Holy Spirit energises us to will and work for His good pleasure.[7] When we sense Jesus in our work and know that it brings pleasure to God, we will count it as a privilege to work with Him, no matter what type of work we do.

Blessing and Curse

Galatians 3:13-14

Christ redeemed us from the curse of the law by becoming a curse for us—for it is written, "Cursed is everyone who is hanged on a tree"—so that in Christ Jesus the blessing of Abraham might come to the Gentiles, so that we might receive the promised Spirit through faith.

At the cross, Jesus redeemed us from every curse by completely destroying sin itself—the source of every curse. As we repent and turn in faith to Him, He exchanges His blood for ours, and takes our curse of spiritual death and gives us the blessing of His love in return.

Scripture says that Jesus became sin so that we might become the righteousness of God in Him.[8] In other words, Jesus took on our sin and destroyed our flesh nature so that we can become the living expression of His love in the world. As we let the love and blessing of God flow through us, the world around us will begin to change and flourish. And it will all be to God's great glory.

Write

If you sense the Lord speaking to you about dealing with generational curses, write a list of all the negative behaviours you see in your family by observation. Look at your parents, grandparents, children, relatives, and yourself. Note down any obvious sins, curses, occultic involvement, habits or addictions, common experiences of trauma or misfortune, emotional shutdown, and any repeating lack of love. Also, ask the Holy Spirit to reveal any hidden generational sin or curse and write down any thoughts He gives you.

Pray

Once you have finished your list, confess the sins you have written down and humble yourself before God. You do not need to do a separate full prayer for each one, but it is helpful to confess each sin out loud.

> *Dear Father, I humble myself before you now to confess my iniquity and the iniquity of my ancestors. I ask for the gift of true repentance—the grace of a transformed heart that turns from what is evil and embraces what is good. Let these be more than words, let them be truth spoken from my heart.*
>
> *I confess the sins of [read out your list]. I repent of these sins. I renounce them and reject them from my life. I break every agreement with these sins and cancel any legal right the enemy has to afflict me in these areas. I revoke all permission given to the enemy through these sins and in the name of Jesus, I expel any demons that are attached to these curses.*
>
> *I thank you Lord for the gift of forgiveness and the power of your blood to break every curse and to cleanse me from all sin and to consume all iniquity. Let your blood wash over my history, cleansing my bloodline and making me innocent and pure in your sight. Let every effect of these sins, both in my life and in the lives of others, be utterly undone and let every curse be turned into a blessing. Please completely purify my heart that I might be a spotless bride, completely devoted to you in wholehearted love.*

Having given these sins and curses to the cross, ask the Lord what He would like to give you in exchange for them.

21 | The Fight of Faith

God only does what He wills. Every action of God works towards His highest will of bringing people into wholehearted love and unity with Him. From evangelism to discipleship and fellowship, the Spirit of God is constantly working to fulfil His design of love. However, the enemy is also always at work, trying to keep people from experiencing God's design for their lives.

Knowing the Enemy

> 2 Corinthians 2:10-11 (BSB)
> If you forgive anyone, I also forgive him. And if I have forgiven anything, I have forgiven it in the presence of Christ for your sake, in order that Satan should not outwit us. For we are not unaware of his schemes.

For thousands of years, it has been said that to win in battle you must know yourself and know your enemy.[1] This is especially true of our spiritual warfare. In order to overcome, we must know ourselves and be confident of our identity in Christ. The Creator and Lord of the Universe lives within us; we are one spirit with Him, and we need to truly believe it.

In the passage above, it was clear that Paul knew his enemy and was aware of the enemy's strategy to use unforgiveness to damage relationships between God's people. He quickly defeats this attack by choosing to forgive. Like Paul, we cannot afford to be ignorant of the enemy's schemes, however, neither can we allow them to distract us. Our call is to seek first the kingdom of God, which means that love is our goal; it is our vision, our mission, and our victory. With this in mind, we do not want to waste time on our enemy.

Instead, we want to keep pursuing our mission of love, but also be ready to deal with the enemy should he ever get in our way.

The enemy's attacks take the form of raids and campaigns. A raid is a quick attack on our thoughts or feelings. A demon of pride might project proud thoughts upon us, or a spirit of fear might make us feel fearful and so on.[2] A key to overcoming raids quickly is to discern the attack as soon as it begins. This is easy when the enemy comes in like a sudden storm. However, sometimes attacks can come like a slowly rising tide of old but familiar thoughts or feelings. If we are to shutdown such subtle raids in their infancy, we need to be aware of our baseline—our usual way of thinking and feeling with Jesus. Our baseline is one of love, humility, faith, joy, optimism, and peace. Any time there is a change, no matter how slight, we need to identify the source and deal with it. If a demonic spirit is behind the attack, we need to stand firm and overcome the enemy through the blood of Jesus, the word of our testimony, and the authority of His name. *In the name of Jesus, with His authority and by the power of His blood, I command this attack to cease! I command every spirit of _____ to leave right now and not come back. I have been crucified with Christ and it is no longer I who live, so the Spirit of Jesus Christ within me declares: Go!*[3]

Campaign Strategies

In addition to quick raids, the enemy also employs more complex strategies in campaigns that can unfold over weeks, months or even years. The diagram on the next page represents one such strategy. The enemy starts by isolating us from God and from other believers. He then brings discouragement, followed by temptation. The enemy then tries to shape our response to the temptation by either leading us to give in to the temptation or by pressuring us to strive our way back to God through legalism. Either of these directions leads us deeper into a spiral of attack and ultimately into defeat.

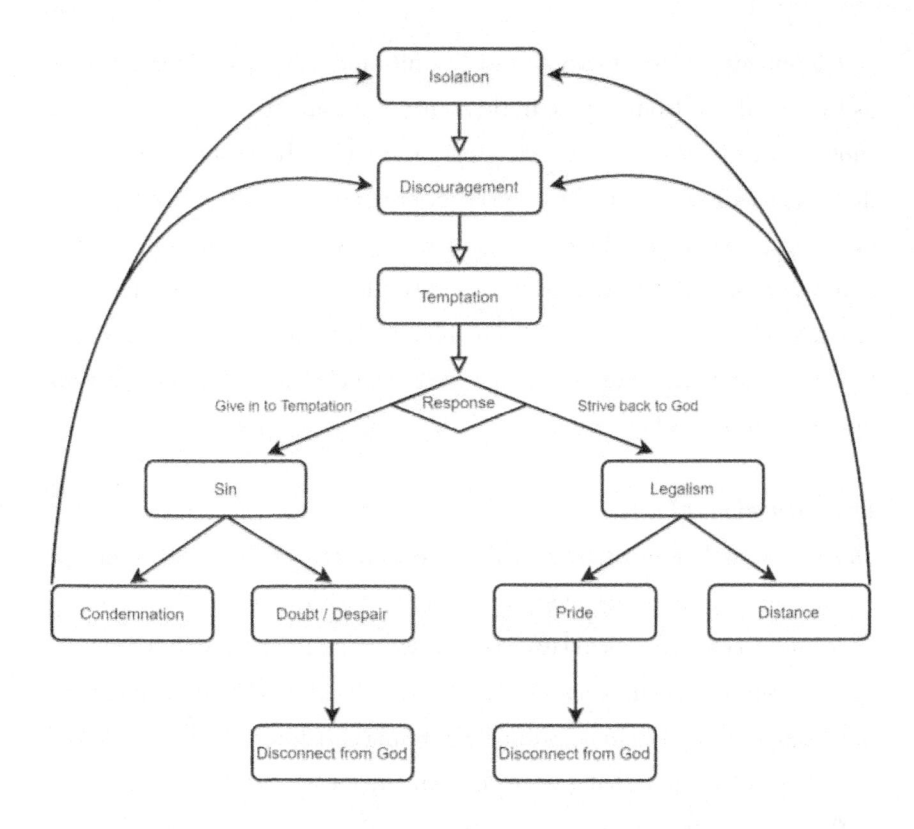

Isolation

Proverbs 18:1
He who isolates himself pursues selfish desires; he rebels against all sound judgment.

All life flourishes in design and languishes outside it. This is especially true for us. God has created us to be channels of His love for Jesus and when we live in this design, we find life in abundance: spiritual prosperity, strength, beauty, significance and joy. Conversely, when we live outside our design, we become spiritually poor, weak and insignificant.

The Father's love for Jesus flows through us as we love one another. This means that *no one* can experience their design of love in isolation. If we are to obey Jesus' command, we need to develop truly loving relationships with other believers. We do not need many, but we do need some.

The enemy understands our need for unity and so his first aim is to isolate us from God and from others. In this stage of the attack, he tries to create a subtle sense of distance in our relationship with God. It may become hard to discern His voice or sense His presence. We may start to feel like God has passed us by or we have done something wrong. At the same time, the enemy may use a project, work, ministry, a misunderstanding, or an offence to separate us from those we love. Something important comes up and we get too busy to connect. Like a solider on the battlefield, we are lured away from our army into No Man's Land.

Discouragement

Once separated from the rest of the army, we are not met with ranks of enemy soldiers, but rather a lone agent. His name is *Discouragement,* and his mission is to persuade us to lay down our weapons and take off our armour.

The spirit of discouragement will often soften us for an attack by targeting our sleep or putting us in emotionally draining situations. We need to know that sleep is a weapon that gives us mental and emotional strength. If we do not use this weapon, as soon as we are physically tired or emotionally weak, the enemy will launch his attack.[4] He always attacks indirectly, composing every lie to start with "I" so that we think these thoughts are coming from our own heart. *"I am alone. No one truly loves me. I fail so often; I'm not even worth being loved. There's no point to doing anything. There's no fruit in my life."* When we take ownership of these thoughts, they become our own doubts to process rather than arrows of the enemy to extinguish.

If we agree with these thoughts, we give permission to the emotions of discouragement to fill our hearts. We start to feel dejected, hopeless, and pessimistic. As we dwell in these emotions, our spiritual strength fades and the thoughts of the enemy sound even more reasonable. If we continue to accept these thoughts, we become even more discouraged and continue to spiral downwards.

No one can be full of faith and discouraged at the same time. So in this stage of the attack, we must choose between faith and discouragement. The moment we accept discouragement, we choose to lay down our shield of faith. We take off the breastplate of faith and love, and the helmet of hope soon follows. As we dwell on the lies of the enemy, we take off the belt of truth and throw down our sword of the word of God. In this place of discouragement, the last thing we feel like is sharing the gospel, and so we take off our shoes as well. And there we stand on the battlefield—naked, defenceless, and alone.

Then the real attack comes.

Temptation

The enemy knows each one of us well. He knows our strengths and weaknesses, and where we have fallen in our old life. So he sends in a familiar spirit to offer relief from the pain of discouragement. This spirit usually tempts us to escape into a sin that has given us a sense of refuge in the past such as over-indulgence in food, media, shopping, entertainment, internet, gaming, or work. If discouragement has left us particularly weak, the enemy may even try a stronger temptation such as drugs, alcohol, pornography, self-harm, or some other addictive habit.

The goal of this temptation is not simply to draw us into sin, but to undermine our identity and holiness in Christ. The enemy knows that what we gain by faith, we maintain by faith. So if he can cause us to doubt the death of our sinful nature, then he can start to rebuild his nature within us. The enemy therefore challenges our identity with thoughts such as, *"Did God really take away all your sin? Then why are you thinking such thoughts and feeling this way? This lust, this pride, this envy—it is all coming from your own heart. The work isn't finished. You're still selfish, insecure and sinful. You'll always be a sinner."*[5]

The enemy wants us to think that being tempted is proof that God has not circumcised our hearts.[6] It is not. Like hearing someone shout profanity at us, it is not a sin *at all* to hear the words that someone else speaks. Nor is it a sin to encounter the thoughts and feelings of a demonic spirit. Jesus heard the voice of the enemy often and in many different ways. But He knew His own heart and He knew His Father. He was tempted in every way and He never once doubted His identity or gave in. And He lives within us!

Our response to this temptation determines the enemy's next move. If we turn to God in the face of the temptation, the enemy will tempt us to strive our way back to Him. We will think that we have to pray for hours or fast or worship our way back to God. By trying to earn our intimacy with God, we fall into legalism and only end up distancing ourselves from God.[7]

If we do not turn to God but give in to the temptation, the enemy then strikes again. He tells us to hide our sin from others, which further isolates us. He then comes against us with condemnation, guilt and shame, accusing us with thoughts like, *"You have done a terrible thing! You are a hypocrite! How could God ever love you? You should weep in misery over the selfish, sinful, pitiful condition of your soul!"* Again, all these thoughts make sense to the natural mind so we agree with them, but this only allows the emotions of condemnation to overwhelm us. These emotions bring with them an ungodly sense of remorse. We grieve over our sin as if it is unforgiven, unwashed, and still present within our soul. Like a wayward child, instead of running back to the embrace of our Father, we lock ourselves in our room and weep, wondering how our Father could ever take us back. In this place, our remorse separates us further from God than our sin ever could. Instead of leading us back to God, it causes us to wallow in unbelief and close our hearts to His unfailing love and goodness.

If we fall deep into despair, the enemy may tempt us to believe that we have disqualified ourselves from the love of God, even to the point of losing His gift of salvation. In their distress, some people feel so unworthy that they walk away from God at this point. Yet no amount of sin can disqualify us from His love for Jesus came specifically for sinners.[8] By acknowledging our sin, we accept that we are the exact target of His love and undeniably qualified for a relationship with Him. Therefore, even if we are unfaithful, Jesus will always remain faithful to His covenant with us. No matter how far we have fallen, Jesus is right there, ready and willing to love us, to take away our sin, and to make us one with Him.

Overcoming

> **Revelation 2:4-7** (NKJV)
>
> "Nevertheless I have this against you, that you have left your first love. Remember therefore from where you have fallen; repent and do the first works, or else I will come to you quickly and remove your lampstand from its place—unless you repent. But this you have, that you hate the deeds of the Nicolaitans, which I also hate. He who has an ear, let him hear what the Spirit says to the churches. To him who overcomes I will give to eat from the tree of life, which is in the midst of the Paradise of God."

Once we are aware of the enemy's plans, we are equipped to overwhelmingly overcome our enemy with Jesus! Here our King reveals one of the most powerful weapons for overcoming: *repentance.*

Overcoming Isolation

Concerning sin, repentance is a change of direction that leads us back to our first love. We must therefore not wait until we consciously fall into sin before we repent. Instead, we need to turn back to God the moment we begin to drift from love. When we find ourselves becoming isolated, we must view isolation as a violation of our design and acknowledge it as a sin. As we accept the instant forgiveness of God and the washing of His blood, we then need to act in repentance by reconnecting with other believers and focusing again on loving Jesus and one another. As we return to loving relationships, our spiritual strength is restored, and we avoid the trap of discouragement.

Overcoming Discouragement

Discouragement is another word for faithlessness. It is not an emotion to process, but a sin to resist. The spirit of discouragement is a real demonic spirit and trying to process the thoughts of discouragement is like having a conversation with someone who wants to kill you. It is far better never to engage at all.[9] Therefore, as soon as we notice thoughts and feelings that draw us downwards into discouragement, we need to repent and break every agreement with the enemy. Once our agreements are broken, the enemy has no right to fill our hearts with the emotions of discouragement. We can then stand in faith, keep our armour on, repel the attack, and maintain our place in the army.

As part of the attack of discouragement, the enemy may directly challenge our holiness in Christ. To defend against this, we need to be confident that the work God has done in circumcising our hearts is real and complete. To help with this, God will confirm His finished work.[10] Once we hear His voice, we can then stand in the confidence of Christ.

Overcoming Temptation

When we are faced with temptation, we must put our trust in Jesus for our overcoming. It is His name that has all authority, and it is His blood that overcomes the enemy. Our part is to enforce the victory that He has won. This can be difficult in the midst of emotion, but we need to remember that there is always a way out and we are not called to fight alone.[11] We can connect with one another and help each other overcome.

If we somehow give in to temptation, we must repent and immediately return to the loving arms of our Father. He does not require a certain level of tears or remorse before He is willing to forgive us. We do not need to work ourselves into a state of distress, hoping that our remorse will somehow inspire God to take pity on us and forgive us.[12] In fact, no emotion is needed at all. Repentance is a decision to turn away from sin and return to our design of love. We can be sure that the very moment we repent, the blood of Jesus completely cleanses us once more and restores us back to our life of love.

Pray

Jesus, thank you for the victory of the cross and the power of your blood that flows through me. Help me to stand in unity with you and fight in your power with your authority. Be my armour Lord; be my righteousness, my hope, my faith, my word. and my truth. Let us fight and overcome the enemy together!

22 | All Authority

Colossians 2:11-15
In him also you were circumcised with a circumcision made without hands, by putting off the body of the flesh, by the circumcision of Christ, having been buried with him in baptism, in which you were also raised with him through faith in the powerful working of God, who raised him from the dead. And you, who were dead in your trespasses and the uncircumcision of your flesh, God made alive together with him, having forgiven us all our trespasses, by cancelling the record of debt that stood against us with its legal demands. This he set aside, nailing it to the cross. He disarmed the rulers and authorities and put them to open shame, by triumphing over them in him.

When Jesus died on the cross, He destroyed the power of sin and in doing so He disarmed all the powers and principalities of darkness.[1] His victory is now ours. Our enemy is defeated and because Jesus lives within us, we have the authority to enforce that defeat and destroy every work of the enemy.

Dealing with Demonic Bondages in Others

Jesus loved people by meeting their needs in every sphere of life. He met physical needs by feeding the hungry, healing the sick, and giving to the poor. He met people's social needs by restoring the outcasts and lifting up the humble. He met the need for education by teaching people, and He met the need for leadership by becoming a servant. Jesus also met people's spiritual needs. When a person needed to be set free from a demon, Jesus did not try to counsel them out of the demon. Rather, He loved them by casting the demon out. He never feared demons, nor did He ignore them. He dealt with them directly as part of sharing His love and healing with people.

Matthew 10:5-10

These twelve Jesus sent out, instructing them, "Go nowhere among the Gentiles and enter no town of the Samaritans, but go rather to the lost sheep of the house of Israel. And proclaim as you go, saying, 'The kingdom of heaven is at hand.' Heal the sick, raise the dead, cleanse lepers, cast out demons. You received without paying; give without pay. Acquire no gold or silver or copper for your belts, no bag for your journey, or two tunics or sandals or a staff, for the labourer deserves his food."

Like the disciples, Jesus sends us into the world to love as He loves—by meeting people's needs. Jesus makes it clear that as we minister with Him, we are not to charge anyone because God's love is *never* for sale. Love always gives freely.

Jesus saw perfectly in both the natural and the spiritual realms. He could tell when someone needed physical healing and when they needed spiritual deliverance. He could also hear the voice of the Holy Spirit clearly, so He always knew what the Father was doing.

Jesus showed us that there is so more to life than just matter, space and time. The physical world exists within a greater spiritual reality and is constantly affected by the spiritual realm. When we live according to the flesh nature, our primary awareness comes from what we sense in the natural realm—what we see, hear, taste, feel, and smell. However, when we are born again, our spirit comes alive in union with the Holy Spirit and our spiritual senses are awakened. Our spirit then communicates what is happening in the spiritual realm to our mind through intuition or discernment.[2]

Like the believers of the early church, it is essential that we learn how to live in the spirit by training our senses to discern the spiritual realm. This does not mean that we look for demons in every corner or attribute everything that is happening in the natural realm to demons or angels. It simply means that we discern what is happening in the natural *and* the spiritual realms. We then listen for the voice of God and respond to each situation in the loving authority of Christ.

My wife Melanie and I coached junior basketball teams for several years. One day, Melanie took a team for a practice. It was their first year and they were learning to dribble the ball. It came time for a girl called Pip to take her turn, but she refused to dribble to the first line.

"I can't do it." She was adamant that she could not dribble the ball.

"Sure you can. I've seen you dribble before. You can do it," Melanie responded.

"I can't do it." For some reason Pip was unmoved by Melanie's encouragement.

"You can. Repeat after me: I can do it!"

"I CAN'T do it!"

"You know that's a lie, right? Do you want to believe a lie?" Melanie did not feel like giving in, but neither did Pip.

"I CAN'T DO IT!" The look in Pip's eyes and her own discernment told Melanie that there was an underlying spiritual dynamic at work. She guided Pip to the back of the line and whispered under her breath, *"In the name of Jesus I bind a lying spirit over this girl."* As soon as Melanie spoke the words, Pip instantly brightened and looked up at her. Her face and her tone had completely changed.

"Can I dribble the ball to the second line?" she asked enthusiastically.

"Sure you can. Go for it!"

Instead of ignoring the hints of what was happening in the spirit, Melanie had discerned the presence of a lying spirit that was constantly feeding lies into this beautiful girl's mind.[3] As soon as Melanie responded in authority, the power of the lie was broken, and Pip was free to believe the truth. We suspected that Pip had become captive to a lying spirit when she agreed with lies that had been spoken over her. For the rest of the season, we constantly spoke truth, love and encouragement over her. The change was dramatic. It was what she needed at that stage of her journey.

Our enemy is merciless and constantly targets children for bondage, often through trauma. As parents, we need to fight for our children and equip them for the battle. When our daughter Keziah was around eight years old, she started to experience fear and anxiety. After some time, we talked with her and she shared how everywhere she looked she saw the word *cancer*. She was terrified that God was telling her she was going to die from cancer. After talking it through, she realised that a spirit of fear was attacking her. She took authority over it and began to take her thoughts captive. The breakthrough was immediate, but the demon did not give up. Within days, Keziah was talking to a friend, who said to her, "You know Keziah, you have the type of skin that would get cancer." Because the demon could not get direct access to Keziah's thoughts, it was targeting her friends, determined to get a foothold of fear in her life. Though upset, Keziah could see it as a spiritual attack, and even at her young age, she took authority with Jesus and overcame it.

> **John 14:10-11**
> "Do you not believe that I am in the Father and the Father is in me? The words that I say to you I do not speak on my own authority, but the Father who dwells in me does his works. Believe me that I am in the Father and the Father is in me, or else believe on account of the works themselves."

Because we live in unity with Jesus, even as children, we share His power and authority. So when we speak to a demon or command healing to sickness, we do not speak in our own authority, but rather the Spirit of Jesus speaks through us. Apart from Jesus, we are nothing and can do nothing. But as we follow His voice, the love of Christ can flow through us with the full force of His power.

If we would only believe that the Spirit of Jesus lives within us, we would realise that we do not need to be a celebrity Christian, an ordained leader, or have some special gifting before we can cast out demons or perform miracles. God is alive within us and He can do His work through us. Our part is simply to act in faith as a channel for His miraculous love. He will do the rest.

Set Free to Receive
> **Timothy 2:24-26** (BSB)
> And a servant of the Lord must not be quarrelsome, but must be kind to everyone, able to teach, and forbearing. He must gently reprove those who oppose him, in the hope that God may grant them repentance leading to a knowledge of the truth. Then they will come to their senses and escape the snare of the devil, who has taken them captive to his will.

Apart from Jesus, all people live in their flesh to varying degrees, which makes them subject to the enemy to do his will. Just as we become agents for the will of God when we live in the Spirit, so we are agents for the will of Satan when we live in the flesh nature.

The agreements that people make with their sinful nature often create partnerships with demons. These demons then actively flood people with sinful thoughts and feelings that keep them from experiencing their design of love. But they can only remain by permission, which is why repentance is so powerful. When a person repents, they break all their agreements with the enemy in that area and revoke all permission for the enemy to operate. The demons then have to leave. However, if the bondage is particularly strong, the people may struggle to repent. In that case, we can help by binding the demons so a person can be set free to turn to God.

Two friends once shared a story with me that beautifully illustrates this point.[4] Ray and Mark often met together to share their spiritual lives and encourage one another. Mark was married to Wendy, a woman who had been spiritually wounded and was bitterly closed to God. Often when Ray came to visit, Wendy would openly mock their conversations about God. Eventually, Ray lost his patience and turned to Wendy.

"In the name of Jesus, I bind everything in you that is stopping you from giving your life to Christ!" That was all it took to set Wendy free enough to repent. Within minutes, she gave her life back to God.

Every single believer has the authority in Christ to set people free and it is easy. Deliverance does not have to be spectacular, confrontational or scary.

A person can be set free from a lifetime of bondage with a simple whisper that is spoken with the authority of Christ. *In Jesus' name, I expel fear from your life. I break the power of lust over your life in the name of Jesus. I command all unforgiveness to go in Jesus' name. Be free to love!*

A New Creation

When a person is under a demonic bondage, it is easy to bind the demon or cast it out. However, we cannot cast out a person's selfish nature. That can only be dealt with as they are crucified with Christ. So how do we relate to someone who is an infant in Christ and still living according to their selfish nature?[5]

> 2 Corinthians 5:16-21
>
> From now on, therefore, we regard no one according to the flesh. Even though we once regarded Christ according to the flesh, we regard him thus no longer. Therefore, if anyone is in Christ, he is a new creation. The old has passed away; behold, the new has come. All this is from God, who through Christ reconciled us to himself and gave us the ministry of reconciliation; that is, in Christ God was reconciling the world to himself, not counting their trespasses against them, and entrusting to us the message of reconciliation. Therefore, we are ambassadors for Christ, God making his appeal through us. We implore you on behalf of Christ, be reconciled to God. For our sake he made him to be sin who knew no sin, so that in him we might become the righteousness of God.

Everyone who follows Jesus is a new creation, created in the image of God. And Jesus is the image of God.[6] Every believer has a unique unity with Jesus, but until they have been crucified with Christ, they also have a sinful nature that lives within them. Our call is to relate to all people for who they are in Christ. As ambassadors for Jesus, we need to inspire people to leave their selfish infancy and pursue the maturity that comes through selfless love.

While people are in their infancy, they will have times when they act selfishly. They may lash out in anger at us, mock us or even harm us. But we need to remember, their sinful behaviour is not them. When people do things to us that they really do not want to do, it is actually their sinful nature that does it, not their new-creation self. Our part is to recognise this and be quick to forgive and to call them into their design of love. This does not mean that we tolerate the flesh nature in one each other in any way. The flesh will always be a cancer that needs destroying, not a mindset that needs our counselling.

The flesh lusts after sympathy and attention, and in their infancy, many believers will feed on any pity and time we give them. They may try to manipulate us, demanding that we pander to their needs as proof of our love. They will then get offended with us when we do not bow to their flesh or love them as they want to be loved. However, our devotion to the first command means that we must not fear offence or be swayed by emotional threats. Instead, we must always seek to love people by meeting their real needs. And a person's ultimate need is to come into their design of love. If we give the flesh what it wants, we will only distract them from their design, add to that person's bondage, keep them in infancy, and lose precious time. There is a far better way.

> **Colossians 1:13-14**
> He has delivered us from the power of darkness and conveyed us into the kingdom of the Son of His love, in whom we have redemption through His blood, the forgiveness of sins.

Jesus delivers people *out of* the powers of darkness and *into* the kingdom of His love. Bringing people into their design of love is Jesus' ultimate goal and so it must govern the way we relate to people and provide the context for all healing and deliverance. We break the power of the enemy over people's lives not merely to end the bondage, but to set people free to fall in love with Jesus. We then help people to go on the journey to the cross to be crucified with Christ, not simply so they can be free from their selfishness, but so they can live in greater love and unity with Jesus.

When people come out of darkness and begin to truly get to know Jesus, not only will they discover their greatest joy in life, but they will also start to share the Father's love for Jesus. And this is where the real glory is found, where Jesus Himself receives blessing beyond imagination!

Pray

Father, thank you for bringing me out of darkness and into your light. Please help me to become aware of the spiritual realm. Open the eyes of my heart to see what you are doing and to hear your voice more clearly. Help me to act in the authority of Christ to bring freedom and love to people. Please help me to see the Spirit of Jesus in your people. Let your love for Jesus burn within me and compel me to meet their needs and call them into their design of love.

23 | Overpowering Principalities

Ephesians 6:10-13
Finally, be strong in the Lord and in the strength of his might. Put on the whole armour of God, that you may be able to stand against the schemes of the devil. For we do not wrestle against flesh and blood, but against the rulers, against the authorities, against the cosmic powers over this present darkness, against the spiritual forces of evil in the heavenly places. Therefore take up the whole armour of God, that you may be able to withstand in the evil day, and having done all, to stand firm.

There are different ranks within the kingdom of darkness, and different spheres of life in which we must overcome them. In the last two chapters, we looked at how to deal with attacks on a personal level and how to deal with demons when they hold other people in bondage. In this chapter, we will look at how to stand against the forces of darkness when they hold positions of authority over entire regions.

1 Timothy 6:11-12 (NKJV)
But you, O man of God, flee these things and pursue righteousness, godliness, faith, love, patience, gentleness. Fight the good fight of faith, lay hold on eternal life, to which you were also called and have confessed the good confession in the presence of many witnesses.

2 Corinthians 10:4-6
For the weapons of our warfare are not of the flesh but have divine power to destroy strongholds. We destroy arguments and every lofty opinion raised against the knowledge of God, and take every thought captive to obey Christ, being ready to punish every disobedience, when your obedience is complete.

Our fight is a fight of faith, and the primary battleground is the mind. Earlier, we saw how the enemy attacks us personally with thoughts that isolate us, discourage us, tempt us, and challenge our unity with Jesus. But God has given us the weapons we need to overcome. Love and unity are two of these weapons, and they are essential at every level of warfare.

As soldiers in a battle, we are not called to fight alone. Often we can assume that because Jesus lives within us, we should be able to overcome every attack of the enemy by ourselves. However, Scripture is clear: we are all parts of a body, woven together in love. And in the same way that we need each other to function as a body, we also need each other to overcome as an army.

We can see this in the way worldly armies work. All armies are organised in a hierarchy, with different groups having different skills and functions. In modern warfare, the basic unit within an army is a team, made up of two or three soldiers. These teams join to form squads, and squads combine to make sections. Sections join together to form platoons, which then combine to form companies, then battalions, then regiments and so on, up to whole armies. It has been said that soldiers are trained to fight first and foremost for the life of the men in their team: the one or two soldiers by their side.

Morale for Battle

Hebrews 3:13

But encourage one another day after day, as long as it is still called "Today," so that none of you will be hardened by the deceitfulness of sin.

Hebrews 10:23-25

Let us hold fast the confession of our hope without wavering, for he who promised is faithful. And let us consider how to stir up one another to love and good works, not neglecting to meet together, as is the habit of some, but encouraging one another, and all the more as you see the Day drawing near.

One of the most valuable yet overlooked forms of love is encouragement. Scripture calls us to meet together and encourage one another day after day so that we will not fall into sin. The Greek word translated as *encourage* is relational in nature and has the sense of encouraging one another *from the place of intimacy*.[1] This need for intimacy is the reason Jesus builds His army upon teams of two or three.[2] He knows that love flows strongest in the smallest numbers. In these groups, we can be more real and vulnerable with one another, which allows more love to flow. The more we live in the light together, the less the powers of darkness can affect us. The more vulnerable we are with each other, the less vulnerable we are to the enemy. And the more we love one another, the more devastatingly powerful we become in the spirit.

If meeting for encouragement is God's command to keep us safe from sin, we can be sure that Satan's command to his demons is the opposite: *"Discourage them day after day! Keep them from meeting together so they cannot encourage one another! Isolate them and cause them to quietly rebel. Then discourage them and swamp them with doubts! Cause them to question the love of God and to disqualify themselves from his goodness! Then watch their hearts harden and their faith fail. Tempt them to sin and then heap shame, condemnation and guilt upon them. Make a mire of regret for them to wallow in."*

God clearly wants better things for us which is why He gives us the insight we need to overcome. In these passages from Hebrews, God shows us how He made us to be fuelled by mutual encouragement. This is not just for our own spiritual growth. As soldiers in Christ, we are called to fight the good fight, and encouragement is our morale for battle.

Authority and Government
Luke 7:2-10
Now a centurion had a servant who was sick and at the point of death, who was highly valued by him. When the centurion heard about Jesus, he sent to him elders of the Jews, asking him to come and heal his

servant. And when they came to Jesus, they pleaded with him earnestly, saying, "He is worthy to have you do this for him, for he loves our nation, and he is the one who built us our synagogue." And Jesus went with them. When he was not far from the house, the centurion sent friends, saying to him, "Lord, do not trouble yourself, for I am not worthy to have you come under my roof. Therefore I did not presume to come to you. But say the word, and let my servant be healed. For I too am a man set under authority, with soldiers under me: and I say to one, 'Go,' and he goes; and to another, 'Come,' and he comes; and to my servant, 'Do this,' and he does it." When Jesus heard these things, he marvelled at him, and turning to the crowd that followed him, said, "I tell you, not even in Israel have I found such faith." And when those who had been sent returned to the house, they found the servant well.

This centurion understood the nature of authority. Everyone who is under authority *must* obey. In the spiritual realm, every demonic spirit is under the authority of Christ and therefore must obey Him. When Jesus speaks through us, they must leave.

In Scripture, all the demons instantly obeyed Jesus, but this was not the case with His disciples. They did not move in the full authority of Christ. This is because our level of spiritual authority is connected to the depth of our unity with Jesus and our level of obedience to Him. The more we become one with Christ and the more we obey His voice, the greater authority we have over the powers of darkness.

Ephesians 2:4-7
But God, being rich in mercy, because of the great love with which he loved us, even when we were dead in our trespasses, made us alive together with Christ—by grace you have been saved— and raised us up with him and seated us with him in the heavenly places in Christ Jesus, so that in the coming ages he might show the immeasurable riches of his grace in kindness toward us in Christ Jesus.

Jesus shares His authority with us not just to win battles against the enemy, but to spiritually govern the world with Him. Every community, region and nation is designed to prosper under the spiritual government of the body of Christ.

Like the elders at the gates, we are seated in heavenly places and have the authority to bind the powers of darkness and release the blessings of God in our communities. However, the body of Christ has been so divided and distracted that we have not possessed the gates of our lands. Instead of taking up our role of spiritual governance, too many of us have fallen for the lie that only a political party can restore righteousness to a nation. We have then focused our energy on promoting the right party, and for many people this has dominated their thinking and conversation far more than the King and His kingdom!

If we look at society through a spiritual lens, we will realise that no secular government can *ever* lead a nation to righteousness. The reason for this is that all the problems in society stem from the flesh nature in people working in partnership with demonic powers. Because love must be freely given and freely received, God Himself cannot force people to love. Instead, He invites us to choose between life or death, love or selfishness. In the same way, no government can force people to embrace their design of love. On the contrary, worldly governments are based on legalism and control, and this gives them only three mechanisms to shape society: education, incentives, and the threat of punishment. Education and incentives are used by governments to get their citizens to act positively. To limit the destructive expressions of people's flesh nature, governments use the threat of punishment. Wherever this threat is removed, we see the selfish nature unleashed and people start hoarding, stealing, abusing, and destroying one another. The painful truth is that no government can deliver people from their selfish nature or fill their hearts with love. And if a government cannot lead a single person into their design as an individual, we can be sure that they cannot lead a whole society into its corporate design.

The battle against the spiritual powers of darkness is the same. Most secular governments deny the spiritual dynamics of life and instead view every problem as a situation that can be solved with policy and money. By ignoring the forces of darkness, those in government are defenceless against their influence, regardless of which side of the political spectrum they fall. Unless they have a strong relationship with Jesus, they will almost certainly partner with these dark powers to shape the laws and culture of society.

People only look to worldly governments to lead them because they can see no other solution. But if people understood the spiritual dynamics that are truly shaping our corporate lives, they would cry out for the body of Christ to take back the gates of the land. We alone have the power to displace the demonic principalities that are currently dominating our communities. And if we are to answer this cry, we must come together and act in corporate spiritual authority.

Corporate Authority

All of us have spheres of spiritual authority that extend over our families and communities. When we discern the enemy at work, it may not be a personal attack on us, but an attack on people within our sphere of authority.

Recently Melanie was having a text conversation with someone who was deeply offended. I realised that this was the third person in just a few days who was struggling with offence.

"Do you think there is a spirit of offence working within our sphere?" I asked Melanie. We decided to take just a minute together to govern our sphere. *In the name of Jesus, through the power of His blood, and with the full authority of His love, we bind a spirit of offence from attacking anyone within our sphere. We expel all offence from our midst and instead release a spirit of love and reconciliation.* The change was immediate. As we finished praying, the next message came through, completely free of offence.

While we have seen the positive effects of governing, we have also seen the impact of not governing well. I remember one time where I discerned an attack of adultery. Although I absolutely trusted Melanie, I assumed that the attack was directed at our marriage. So I prayed and resisted the attack. However, I did not realise this was actually an attack within our sphere. That night, one of the people close to us ended up being seduced into committing adultery. If we had only effectively governed our sphere, so much pain could have been so easily avoided.

God is calling us all to a life of great consequence, but with this comes great responsibility. Other people will feel the effects of our failure to govern. Therefore we need to learn how to both fight and govern within our sphere of authority. The begins with praying and then acting to see God's design of love established, not just in our lives as individuals, but in our marriages, our families, communities, cities, regions and ultimately entire nations.

The fruit of the fight was enjoyed by Pip in the last chapter. As soon as that lying spirit was bound, she was instantly free to embrace the truth. The same was true for Wendy; as soon as the spirit of offence was bound, she was set free to give her life back to Jesus. It will be exactly the same for an entire society. As soon as we all start to govern our spheres, the powers of darkness that presently reign over our lands will be overcome and people will be free to receive God's love. Therefore, by calling His people to possess the gates of authority, God is preparing the world for a massive harvest of souls.

> **Matthew 13:47**
> "Again, the kingdom of heaven is like a net that was thrown into the sea and gathered fish of every kind."

The kingdom of God is like a net that gathers fish for the harvest. Because the kingdom of God is governed by the laws of love, if we want to participate in the harvest then we need to live by these laws. No king sends a rebellious and self-willed ambassador out to represent him, fight for him, or govern on his behalf. Instead, he invests his authority in those who are loyal and fully aligned with his will. It is the same for us. Our spiritual authority and right to govern is connected to our loyalty and obedience.

Obedience always starts with the most important commands, and our obedience to Jesus starts with the new command: to love one another. This command means that no one person can displace a demonic principality or take the gates of a community alone because no one can be fully obedient to God on their own. We can only love one another with one another.

The Holy Spirit is now bringing His people together like an army of countless thousands of small groups. He is releasing the oil of His anointing and energising us to love Jesus through one another and to become one in Him.[3] As His love flows in these groups, our obedience will elevate us to the place of authority where we can truly displace our enemy. Through our combined authority, we will be able to possess the gates and take our place in the spiritual governance of our communities, regions and nations. From this position of power, we can then release the rule and reign of Christ's love in our land. And it will be powerful beyond words.

These same groups that overcome the enemy and possess the gates will become the net that holds the harvest. All love is attractive and as people see our love for one another, they will be drawn like thirsty people to pure waters. When we invite non-believers to our small groups, we can lavish them with the love of God, encourage them, and meet their needs. As they experience God's love and respond to His truth, these people will be woven into the body of Christ. This is how the early church exploded, not by gathering people together in great numbers, but by scattering them in small families of faith and love. This is what this world needs. This is His glory that will cover the earth. This is His Kingdom come.

Pray

Jesus, I thank you that you are the King of Love who sits upon the throne! Thank you that you want to flood our lands with your reign of love. Please help me to be fully obedient to you and to walk in your authority. Show me how to dispossess the enemy and take the gates of our community with other believers. Let the rulers of darkness be cast down in our lands and let your love reign!

24 | Journey of Love

Romans 15:4
For whatever was written in former days was written for our instruction, that through endurance and through the encouragement of the Scriptures we might have hope.

The things that are recorded in the Scriptures are written for our instruction. Throughout Scripture we find symbols or living parables—messages from God woven into the fabric of human experience. While these messages only highlight what is already clear in Scripture, they can help by giving us insight into how God is leading us on this journey into love.

In Chapters Three and Seven of this book, we looked at the journey of Abraham into the Promised Land. Abraham came into covenant with God in stages. In the first stage, God put Abraham into a deep sleep. As Abraham slept, the Father and Son passed between the pieces and moved through the blood together. Jesus made covenant with God on Abraham's behalf.

By walking through the blood, Jesus took responsibility for keeping the covenant and He accepted the penalty of death should we ever break the covenant. Abraham came into this covenant while he was asleep, resting in the work of the Lord. Then, years after first entering covenant with God, Abraham was called into the covenant of circumcision. And this time he was wide awake.

From Egypt to Canaan

We can see the same stages of covenant in the lives of children of Abraham. In keeping with His promise, God gave Abraham and Sarah a son, whom they named Isaac. Isaac had a son called Jacob who was later renamed Israel. Jacob had twelve sons who formed the tribes of Israel. Jacob's entire family moved to Egypt to join his son Joseph and escape a famine. After a time, Joseph and the Pharaoh died, and a new Pharaoh took his place. This Pharaoh enslaved the people of Israel.

After the people had lived a long time in slavery, God then raised up Moses as His messenger to Pharaoh. This was the beginning of a living parable, told in the life of an entire nation. It was their journey into covenant.

> **Exodus 6:6-9**
> "Say therefore to the people of Israel, 'I am the Lord, and I will bring you out from under the burdens of the Egyptians, and I will deliver you from slavery to them, and I will redeem you with an outstretched arm and with great acts of judgment. I will take you to be my people, and I will be your God, and you shall know that I am the Lord your God, who has brought you out from under the burdens of the Egyptians. I will bring you into the land that I swore to give to Abraham, to Isaac, and to Jacob. I will give it to you for a possession. I am the Lord.'" Moses spoke thus to the people of Israel, but they did not listen to Moses, because of their broken spirit and harsh slavery.

God sent Moses to the people of Israel with the promise that He would set the people free and take them to be His own. God would give them a land of their own possession. They would no longer be slaves, forced to endlessly work as machines for their masters. Instead, they would belong to God and He would reign over them in compassion, having made them a people of His own love. But their spirit was so broken by the cruelty of their slavery that no one dared to believe it.

God kept His promise and acted despite the unbelief of His people. Through Moses, He performed a series of signs and wonders, but Pharaoh refused to obey. Finally, God sent the plague of death. The people of Israel sacrificed a lamb and painted their doorposts with its blood, calling the feast "the Passover." The Angel of God passed over the houses that were covered with the blood and instead took the lives of all the firstborns of the families of Egypt, including Pharaoh's firstborn son.

Pharaoh let the people go. They fled, following a pillar of cloud and fire, which brought them to the Red Sea. God then divided the Red Sea, allowing Israel to pass through on dry ground. Pharaoh and his army pursued them into the divide but were drowned when the sea returned to its natural state.

Once through the Red Sea, God led the people of Israel by a pillar of fire and a cloud of smoke through the wilderness of the Sinai Peninsula.

> **Leviticus 18:24-25**
> Do not make yourselves unclean by any of these things, for by all these the nations I am driving out before you have become unclean, and the land became unclean, so that I punished its iniquity, and the land vomited out its inhabitants.

It was in the wilderness that God gave Moses the Torah or Instruction. The people of Israel lived at a time when evil abounded and acts such as child sacrifice were common. Because of the evil, the land of Canaan was spewing out its inhabitants. It was seeking to be possessed by a righteous people. However, the hearts of the people of Israel had been shaped by the world around them. So before they could possess the land, they firstly needed to learn about righteousness and what it really means to be human.

One Great Command

> **Deuteronomy 6:4-5**
> Hear, O Israel: The LORD our God, the LORD is one. You shall love the LORD your God with all your heart and with all your soul and with all your might.

The entire Law was built upon one great command: to love God with all our heart, soul, and strength. This command was closely followed by the second: to love others as ourselves. The rest of the Torah explored the basic principles of a life of love—do not commit incest; do not have sex with animals; do not sacrifice your children; do not murder, rape, slander, hate, exploit or take revenge on people. Instead, love God with your entire being. Follow His voice and live in unity with Him. Love others as if they were you. Honour your parents. Rest on the Sabbath. Lend to those in need and give to the poor. Look after your animals. Provide for vulnerable people. Make things right. Be a blessing to people around you. Celebrate. Pray. Worship. Be honest. Be brave. Be holy.

> **Deuteronomy 10:12-16**
> "And now, Israel, what does the Lord your God require of you, but to fear [revere] the Lord your God, to walk in all his ways, to love him, to serve the Lord your God with all your heart and with all your soul, and to keep the commandments and statutes of the Lord, which I am commanding you today for your good? Behold, to the Lord your God belong heaven and the heaven of heavens, the earth with all that is in it. Yet the Lord set his heart in love on your fathers and chose their offspring after them, you above all peoples, as you are this day. Circumcise therefore the foreskin of your heart, and be no longer stubborn."

Through Moses, God made it clear that the people would find their greatest fulfilment and blessing by living according to His design. Moses knew that it was possible—God was able to do what He had promised to do. So he was understandably frustrated by the people's unbelief. Moses could see that God was offering His dying people life-saving medicine. But he could also see that the people preferred their poison. They had not taken hold of the truth nor believed the promise. They lacked revelation. They were too slow to believe and too stubborn to surrender. And the day was coming when it would be too late. So Moses pleads with them: *It is simple, attainable, and it is for your own good! But you must circumcise your heart and yield your will to God!*

It was never within the power of the people to circumcise their own hearts. It was always going to be an act of God's grace. Moses was simply calling the people to participate with God by faith and give Him permission to change their hearts. However, even though God had set His love and affection on Israel, if the people continued to resist His love, then God would not force it on them. He would let them remain in their unbelief.

And so it was. The people rebelled. They had personally experienced the redeeming power of God. They had seen so many awesome miracles of God, but fear and doubt consumed their heart and destroyed all vision for a life of love. Still God gave them a chance to experience His promise. He led Israel to the edge of the Promised Land and Moses sent out spies. The spies found a land flowing with milk and honey, but one which also contained walled cities and giants. The people of Israel looked to their own ability and chose fear over faith. Just as they had refused their design of love, so now they refused to enter the land. So God sent the people back into the wilderness.

> **Psalm 106:24-27**
> Then they despised the pleasant land,
>   having no faith in his promise.
> They murmured in their tents,
>   and did not obey the voice of the Lord.
> Therefore he raised his hand and swore to them
>   that he would make them fall in the wilderness,
>   and would make their offspring fall among the nations,
>   scattering them among the lands.

Psalm 106 details the ongoing rebellion of the people in the wilderness. They had not left Egypt in their hearts. They remained united with their sinful nature and refused to listen to the voice of God who alone could save them from themselves. Their selfish nature then sabotaged their entire future. It caused them to despise their freedom, reject God's promise, and forfeit the blessing of their inheritance. The people of Israel listened to their fear rather than the voice of God and so chose to die in the wilderness. And that is exactly what happened.

After 40 years in the wilderness, the faithless generations had all passed away, except for Joshua and Caleb. God then led the next generation of His people to cross the Jordan River and enter the Promised Land. The people of Israel crossed over and the men were then circumcised in Gilgal. Then when they had healed, they began their conquest of Jericho and the nations of Canaan. And all of this was written for our instruction and encouragement.

Pray

Father, thank you for the journey that you are taking me on. Please purge me of all fear, doubt and unbelief. Please grant me faith, courage and love to receive your promise and take the Land.

25 | Into the Land

> **1 Corinthians 5:6-7**
> Your boasting is not good. Do you not know that a little leaven leavens the whole lump? Cleanse out the old leaven that you may be a new lump, as you really are unleavened. For Christ, our Passover lamb, has been sacrificed.

The journey of God's people from Egypt to the Promised Land is a living picture of our spiritual journey into a life of abundant love. Just as Israel was enslaved in Egypt, so we were also slaves to our selfish nature and powerless to free ourselves.[1] But because of His great love, the Father saved us through the blood of the Passover Lamb: Jesus Christ. At the cross, Jesus poured out His blood and took the curse of death to save us.

The Passover echoes the first act of covenant in Abraham's life when Jesus made covenant with the Father on Abraham's behalf. God put Abraham into a deep sleep to show us that there is nothing we can ever do to earn our salvation. All we can do is apply His blood through faith to the doorposts of our hearts and rest in the power of the cross. As we place our trust in God, Jesus brings us into a new life of covenant love and unity with Him.

The Red Sea

> **1 Corinthians 10:1-4**
> For I do not want you to be unaware, brothers, that our fathers were all under the cloud, and all passed through the sea, and all were baptised into Moses in the cloud and in the sea, and all ate the same spiritual food, and all drank the same spiritual drink. For they drank from the spiritual Rock that followed them, and the Rock was Christ.

Scripture says that the people of Israel were baptised into Moses in the cloud and in the sea. Passing through the Red Sea speaks of our baptism in water. It is an outward sign that we have been saved by grace from the world of sin and death. Being baptised into the cloud represents being baptised in the Spirit.

The Wilderness

As Israel found in the wilderness, it is easier for us to leave our old life than it is to leave our old self. Even though God has forgiven our sin and we have been baptised in water, the old self still lives within us and continues to influence the way we think and act. As spiritual infants in Christ, we are still self-absorbed, self-governing, self-righteous and constantly self-gratifying. Like little children, we have yet to learn what life is all about.

In our infancy, we have a lot to discover about God, our identity in Christ, and God's design for our life. Yet it can be easy to get distracted by other things. If we are not completely confident in the goodness of God, we will start to focus on the issues of this life: what we will eat, where we will live, what work we will do, and how we will entertain ourselves. In this place, we can naively accept our selfish behaviour as normal. Everyone around us is the same and so together we wander through a spiritual wilderness, seeking wealth and comfort and a measure of meaning. Because we still see God move in power at times, we reassure ourselves by telling each other that this life is normal, even blessed. We pitch our tents, raise our banners, and call our part of the wilderness, *The Promised Land*.

Yet God does not give up on us. He calls us softly: *Come. I have a greater life for you. The cloud has moved on. Come away with Me. Come to a land flowing with milk and honey. Come to a life of love, freedom, and boundless joy. This is a life worth fighting for and dying for. Come away with Me.*

As we take God's hand, He begins to teach us about who we truly are in union with Him. He reveals the nature of the old self and helps us to forge our identity in Christ separate from the flesh. As we continue to grow, we begin to learn more about our design of love. We start to see the first command as the first promise. We realise that God guarantees to circumcise our hearts for one reason: that we may love Him with all our heart. This is what we were created for. Our whole being was perfectly created for love.

When we finally embrace God's design for our life, we arrive at our time of love.

> **Ezekiel 16:7-8** (NKJV)
> "I made you thrive like a plant in the field; and you grew, matured, and became very beautiful. Your breasts were formed, your hair grew, but you were naked and bare. When I passed by you again and looked upon you, indeed your time was the time of love; so I spread My wing over you and covered your nakedness. Yes, I swore an oath to you and entered into a covenant with you, and you became Mine," says the Lord God.
>
> **Jeremiah 2:2**
> Thus says the LORD, "I remember the devotion of your youth, your love as a bride, how you followed me in the wilderness, in a land not sown."

In the wilderness, God gave Israel the Torah, which was His *ketubah* or marriage contract with Israel. In our own spiritual journey, when we say "Yes" to the greatest command, it is like saying "I do" to Jesus. We make a covenant of wholehearted love that commits us to a life of unity with Jesus, and He spreads His wing over us and makes a covenant with us.

Coming into the marriage covenant is coming into the heart of God *for Jesus*. When we first started in our relationship with God, we encountered Jesus as our Redeemer and He presented us to the Father as a child of God. Now, having matured us and brought us to our time of love, the Father presents us back to Jesus as a bride of surpassing beauty. Like the Shulamite, we then come up out of the wilderness, leaning on our beloved.[2]

Crossing the Jordan

When Israel crossed the Jordan River, their wilderness life ended and life in the land began. The Jordan flows down into the Dead sea, and in Hebrew, the word *Jordan* means *Descender*. In spiritual terms, crossing the Jordan river speaks of being baptised into the death of Christ.

> **Romans 6:3-4**
> Do you not know that all of us who have been baptised into Christ Jesus were baptised into his death? We were buried therefore with him by baptism into death, in order that, just as Christ was raised from the dead by the glory of the Father, we too might walk in newness of life.

It is our inheritance to be baptised into death with Jesus so that we might be raised into new life. This baptism does not speak of our physical baptism in water but of a spiritual immersion into the death of Christ.

Death and Circumcision

> **Joshua 5:7**
> So it was their children, whom he raised up in their place, that Joshua circumcised. For they were uncircumcised, because they had not been circumcised on the way.

The first generation of Hebrews had broken the covenant that God made with Abraham and failed to circumcise their hearts and their children. After crossing over the Jordan, Joshua then circumcised all the males of Israel. Through circumcision, the people of Israel were restored into covenant and prepared to take the Land.

> **Colossians 2:11** (NASB)
> In Him you were also circumcised with a circumcision made without hands, in the removal of the body [entirety] of the flesh [selfish nature] by the circumcision of Christ.

Physical circumcision was made by the removal of the foreskin. In Christ, we are spiritually circumcised by the removal of the *entirety* of the flesh nature. This was made possible by Jesus' death on the cross. When Jesus poured out His blood as a sacrifice for sin, He released the awesome power of God to cut the entire selfish nature out of our hearts. And His blood was enough.

Taking the Land

Deuteronomy 7:1-2

"When the Lord your God brings you into the land that you are entering to take possession of it, and clears away many nations before you, the Hittites, the Girgashites, the Amorites, the Canaanites, the Perizzites, the Hivites, and the Jebusites, seven nations more numerous and mightier than you, and when the Lord your God gives them over to you, and you defeat them, then you must devote them to complete destruction. You shall make no covenant with them and show no mercy to them."

After Israel had crossed the Jordan, they had to overcome many nations. Their call was to completely cleanse the land. Why? God created the land to be possessed by righteous people. The nations of Canaan practiced "every abominable thing that the LORD hates," even burning their children in worship to their gods.[3] Therefore the land was expelling its people so it could be possessed by a righteous people. But Israel was subject to the same law. If the people of Israel rejected their design of love, the land would reject them. And so it did.

Like Israel, once we have come through the circumcision of the heart, we still have many battles to fight. The nations that Israel fought represent the temptations of the world around us, the ranks of the powers of darkness in the spiritual realm, and the strongholds of the mind within us.

Renewing the Mind

When they crossed the Jordan, the people of Israel were transformed from desert wanderers into land conquerors. As they entered the land, they had to adjust to their new life, leaving their old ways of thinking behind them. Their old lifestyle, mindsets, perspectives, ways of relating, actions, and their works; everything had to change in the land of their inheritance. They had to be prepared to fight and overcome, to settle lands and build homes, to sow and to reap. A new beginning of fruitfulness and abundance had come.

In the same way, when the selfish nature dies, all of our sinful desires are destroyed, and we can live in freedom with Jesus. But this new life calls for a whole new way of thinking and living. So many of us are taught that the goal of Christianity is to sin less rather than to love more. If we think like this, we can be tempted to believe that being crucified with Christ is the ultimate goal of life. It is not. The death of the flesh nature is simply one step on the journey to a life of wholehearted love, intimacy and unity with God. This is a journey into the infinite nature of God, where only the first few steps are taken in this life. Beyond the removal of our flesh nature, the next steps involve renewing our thinking to align with the truth. We are to no longer think *I* but *We*. We need to test our beliefs, expose lies, and embrace the truth. We need to tear down old strongholds of the mind and create new strongholds of love and humility. We need to learn to sow in love and reap in joy. This requires a renewing of the mind that will continue for the rest of our lives.

Edom Vows to Rebuild

As well as renewing the mind, we must also contend with the enemy. The nation of Edom was founded by Esau, the godless and unholy brother of Jacob.[4] Like Esau, the sin nature is godless and unholy, and so its presence defiles our temple. And just as the nations of Israel and Edom warred against each other, so the spirit and flesh are in constant conflict with each other. One is godly, holy and loving; the other is godless, unholy and selfish.

It is in this light that God loved Jacob but hated Esau, for God loves the Spirit nature within us but hates our selfish nature. And just as God condemned Edom, so He condemns our sinful nature to total destruction.

Malachi 1:1-4

The oracle of the word of the Lord to Israel by Malachi.

"I have loved you," says the LORD. But you say, "How have you loved us?" "Is not Esau Jacob's brother?" declares the LORD. "Yet I have loved Jacob but Esau I have hated. I have laid waste his hill country and left his heritage to jackals of the desert." If Edom says, "We are shattered but we will rebuild the ruins," the LORD of hosts says, "They may build, but I will tear down, and they will be called 'the wicked country,' and 'the people with whom the LORD is angry forever.'"

What God has devastated, Edom vows to rebuild. When God destroys our selfish nature, the enemy vows to rebuild it again. Demonic powers will use every tool of deception and temptation to sow the seed of sin back into our hearts.

As we saw earlier, our call is to stand against every attack of the enemy. We are to abide in our unity with Jesus and speak in His authority to release the power of His blood against our enemy. In the unlikely event that we should ever fall from grace and let the enemy re-sow the selfish nature within us, then we can trust God to keep His promise: if the enemy rebuilds, God will again destroy. He will always do whatever it takes to restore our design as channels of His love.

We can be encouraged that times of battle and testing will always come to an end. If we stand firm against the enemy, we will know the reward of our faith: a heart that is consumed by the fire of God's love.

Pray

Father, thank you that you have prepared a life for me beyond all imagination. Thank you that you can make it possible. Please lead me on the next step into this life of wholehearted love and unity with you. Let me not spend a single moment longer than necessary in the wilderness. Let us take the land together!

26 | Choose Life

Our covenant with Jesus is not a contract that we add to our life, nor is it a certificate of entitlement we can use to demand blessing. It is the defining force of an entirely new life—one that is lived in the design of God.

> **Isaiah 42.6-7**
> "I am the LORD; I have called you in righteousness;
>   I will take you by the hand and keep you;
>   I will give you as a covenant for the people,
>   a light for the nations,
>   to open the eyes that are blind,
>   to bring out the prisoners from the dungeon,
>   from the prison those who sit in darkness."

This prophecy in Isaiah speaks of Jesus coming as a light for the nations to bring the revelation of the Father. God has raised Jesus up to be a covenant for the people. When Jesus made a covenant with the Father on behalf of Abraham, He became our covenant. We now enter into the covenant, not simply by making an agreement with God, but by becoming one with Christ.

For He is your life

> **Deuteronomy 30:19-20a**
> I call heaven and earth to witness against you today, that I have set before you life and death, blessing and curse. Therefore choose life, that you and your offspring may live, loving the LORD your God, obeying his voice and holding fast to him [becoming one with Him], for He is your life…

When treaties or covenants are made between nations, the more powerful nation sets the terms. So when God brings us into covenant, there is no negotiation. God alone sets the terms of our covenant relationship, and He makes them clear.

When we choose to live in covenant with God, we bind ourselves to:
1. Loving Him with our entire being and loving others,
2. Hearing and obeying His voice,
3. And living in unity with Him.

Together these three areas define a covenant life. When we love God, hear His voice and live in union with Him, *God becomes our life.* We share one spirit with Jesus, and it is no longer we who live but Jesus who lives in us. Because of this unity, there can be nothing remotely burdensome about a covenant life. It is a life of exhilarating love, intimacy, and unity. It is a life of great joy, peace and purpose. And it is a life that will last forever.

Psalm 89:28
My steadfast love I will keep for him forever,
    And my covenant will stand firm for him.

The word translated as *steadfast love,* is the Hebrew word *chesed.* Different Bible versions translate chesed in different ways such as kindness, mercy, unfailing love, loyalty, steadfast love and so on. Chesed embodies all these qualities, but at its foundation, chesed is a love that is forged through covenant.

As we learned earlier, when people made a covenant in ancient times, they would accept death as the penalty should they ever break their covenant. However, it was not primarily the fear of death that caused people to keep their covenant to one another. The driving force behind their faithfulness was chesed love.

> **Hebrews 13:20-21** (emphasis added)
> Now may the God of peace who brought again from the dead our Lord Jesus, the great shepherd of the sheep, **by the blood of the eternal covenant**, equip you with everything good that you may do his will, working in us that which is pleasing in his sight, through Jesus Christ, to whom be glory forever and ever. Amen.

Chesed love is defined as "covenant-*loyalty* – pre-eminently, God's perfect loyalty to His own covenant."[1] At the cross, Jesus poured out His blood, made an eternal covenant, and released the full force of God's chesed love. God Himself is now perfectly loyal to this covenant. He can never break this covenant or undo it, nor would He ever want to. For what greater covenant could there ever be beyond the blood of Christ? Absolutely none. The blood of Jesus has created a perfect covenant and it is guaranteed for eternity.

In order to be faithful to His covenant, God must fulfil *every* promise to us. He must provide all our basic needs for the rest of our lives because He promised it and His chesed love guarantees it. We can trust in His protection, His blessing, His voice, His guidance, His presence, and His extravagant goodness, all because of His chesed love. As surely as God is love, He will be faithful to keep His covenant with us *forever*.

> **Proverbs 19:22**
> What is desired in a man is steadfast love [*chesed*],
>   and a poor man is better than a liar.

God longs for His chesed love to live within us so we can be faithful to His covenant. Because Jesus promises to make our obedience possible, if we are willing, God must:

- circumcise the old self from our hearts as He has promised,
- fill every part of our being with His Spirit and love,
- continue to speak to us and help us to cultivate intimacy with Him,
- provide all our needs,
- and sustain our faithfulness by living in unity with us.

God's chesed-love demands all this, and He delights to do it! Jesus is simply waiting for us to give Him the permission He needs to fulfil His covenant promises.

Works vs. Grace

As we learned earlier, we give God our permission to act by devoting our lives to the greatest command. This devotion is a choice that we make by faith and it far surpasses mere intellectual agreement. When we choose life, we do not choose to believe in a life but to live a life of love, intimacy and unity with God. When we make this choice, we embrace total dependency on God. We accept that we cannot fix ourselves. We cannot crucify our own sin nature or restore our design of love. So by faith, we abandon our own efforts and turn to Jesus to keep His promise. And He does not let us down.

The greatest threats to wholehearted love do not come from the old self, but from the theologies of legalism and license, both of which distort the grace of God. Legalism says we must work to earn a blessing and strive to overcome our sinful instincts. License says that we do not need to work at all to be blessed by God. It says that we already have every blessing of God, so our selfish nature is either already overcome or entirely irrelevant. Both of these beliefs lock us out of our inheritance, the first by trying to make us earn an unearnable gift; the second by making us believe that we have already received it.

> **Matthew 11:28-29**
> Come to me, all who labour and are heavy laden, and I will give you rest. Take my yoke upon you, and learn from me, for I am gentle and lowly in heart, and you will find rest for your souls.

The only way to know a life of wholehearted love is to be truly yoked with Jesus. Being yoked with Jesus speaks of finding rest *and* doing work. It is only possible to rest and work when we are in unity with Jesus and He carries the load.

In *First Love,* we look at legalism and the direction of our works. If our works flow *to* God with the purpose of earning anything from Him, they are worthless, burdensome, manipulative, dead, and exhausting. If our works flow *from* God with the purpose of expressing His love, they are restful, life-giving and full of His joy. This is because the Spirit energises us to will and work for His good pleasure.

There was never meant to be a separation of works from faith, grace and love. Without works, our faith is merely a philosophy. Without works, our love is merely sentiment. Paul confirms the place of works when He writes that true grace works incredibly hard—not to earn God's blessing but to express His love.[2] So faith, grace, love and works all exist in a perfect unity that we call relationship with God. This is something that legalism and license can never replace.

Covenant and the Sabbath

Hebrews 4:1-10

Therefore, while the promise of entering his rest still stands, let us fear lest any of you should seem to have failed to reach it. For good news came to us just as to them, but the message they heard did not benefit them, because they were not united by faith with those who listened. For we who have believed enter that rest, as he has said,

"As I swore in my wrath,
'They shall not enter my rest,'"

although his works were finished from the foundation of the world. For he has somewhere spoken of the seventh day in this way: "And God rested on the seventh day from all his works." And again in this passage he said,

"They shall not enter my rest."

Since therefore it remains for some to enter it, and those who formerly received the good news failed to enter because of disobedience, again he appoints a certain day, "Today," saying through David so long afterward, in the words already quoted,

> "Today, if you hear his voice,
> do not harden your hearts."
>
> For if Joshua had given them rest, God would not have spoken of another day later on. So then, there remains a Sabbath rest for the people of God, for whoever has entered God's rest has also rested from his works as God did from his.

In this passage, the Promised Land is used as a symbol of our Sabbath rest. Many commentators believe this is speaking of heaven, and on one level this is surely true, but the writer says that "we who have believed enter that rest." Today there is rest for every believer. It is found in the Promised Land of love and unity with Jesus Christ.

God gave the people of Israel two signs of their covenant with Him: circumcision and observing the Sabbath. These signs set Israel apart from all the other nations of the world. As living symbols, these signs speak of the circumcision of the heart and the rest we find in Jesus as we cease all our striving. Imagine a world in which believers were known for their selfless love and their abiding sense of peace! Imagine the body of Christ, radiating the glory of His love, living in His holiness, and completely free from all stress. Imagine a world in which we are known as Christ's disciples by our unwavering love for one another!

For so long, the Church has tried to appeal to selfish people using attractions and teachings that promote a selfish, infantile Christianity. We have focused on a gospel that makes people more hungry to be blessed than to become a blessing. For so many people, this mix of selfishness and spirituality has led to a desolate experience of the Christian faith. What the world desperately needs to see is life as God designed. It needs to see people who have devoted their lives to wholehearted love and have possessed the land. It needs to see the love of God burning in the eyes of His people. It needs to see the Spirit of Jesus, living in and through His people. It desperately needs to see Christ in you. So today if you hear His voice, do not harden your heart. Come and enter the rest of your life.

Pray

Father, thank you for your chesed-love. Thank you that you will be faithful to every promise. I ask that you share your chesed-love with me and empower me to be faithful to your covenant. Thank you for sharing your yoke with me and making this all possible. It is a gift beyond words. Thank you. I pray that my gratitude would be seen in every act of love that we do together. May our love keep growing stronger forever.

Final Words

Everything in creation finds its greatest pleasure when it lives according to its design. My dog, Sasha, loves to chase small animals because it is a part of her design. When she is on the hunt, she comes alive with energy and focus. She absolutely loves the chase and so does what she is designed to do, not out of a sense of duty, but out of a sense of pure joy. It is the same for us. God has designed us to find our ultimate pleasure and greatest joy by living in His design of selfless love.

> **Song of Solomon 1:2**
> Let him kiss me with the kisses of his mouth!
> For your love is better than wine.

God created us to live in unity with Jesus, one with His consuming love. The love of Christ is passionate and pure; it is intense beyond imagination and spiritually intoxicating. This is the love He wants to share with us.

Likewise, the Father wants to share His love for Jesus with us and make us channels of His love. As we let Him fulfil this design, we will find the greatest joy possible in life. This new life begins as we make a covenant with God, to love Him with our entire being, to hear His voice, and to live in unity with Him. For His sake, *we must choose life!*

Thank You

I consider myself profoundly privileged to have written the *One with Christ* series. I am blessed beyond words that you have invested the time in reading the material. You have helped me to multiply the gold I have been entrusted with and I know that Jesus will delight in receiving the increase. May you now multiply your own gold, investing the love and truth of Christ into those around you and growing ever deeper in His love.

Final Prayer

Father, I pray for every reader of this book, that you would bring them into the fullness of their design as a channel of Your love. Let every fibre of their being burn with Your intense love for Jesus. And may they find their ultimate pleasure as Your love flows through them.

Lord, let the glory of Your love shine through them so brightly that people stand in awe and are drawn to You through them. Help them to always grow in their love and unity with Jesus. May they see with Your vision, think with Your thoughts, feel with Your heart, and act with Your love. May they delight in hearing and obeying Your voice. May each one live as a beautiful bride of Christ, as a fearless warrior in Your army, and as a playful child in Your house. May it bring You incredible pleasure to love Your Son through them and to reveal Jesus in them. May their life bring you constant delight and glory. And may they be forever one with You.

Thank you again for investing the time to grow closer to God through the *One with Christ* books. I look forward to spending time with you in eternity, if not before.

All blessings, life and joy be to you in the love of our Lord Jesus Christ, the grace of our glorious Father, and in the power of His Holy Spirit.

Geoff Woodcock, author – *One with Christ* series.

Connect

If you would like to connect with us, share a testimony, or support our work, please visit our websites below. We would love to hear from you.

Onewithchrist.org
All the books in the *One with Christ* series can be downloaded here for free and print copies are also available for purchase. We also have articles and media that support our design of love.

Oneanother.net
This is a website for connecting small groups of people who are devoted to loving God and loving one another.

Freeslaves.org
As part of our vision to love Jesus by meeting the needs of His people, we redeem enslaved families and provide education and relief to those trapped in poverty and slavery. We would love to invite you to join us and love Jesus through this ministry.

Acaciaprojects.org
The above projects are all run by our main organisation: Acacia Projects. If you would like to get involved with the team at Acacia Projects or support our work, please visit acaciaprojects.org

ONE WITH CHRIST

Now to Him
who is able to keep you from stumbling,
and to make you stand
in the presence of His glory
blameless with great joy,
to the only God our Saviour,
through Jesus Christ our Lord,
be glory, majesty, dominion and authority,
before all time and now and forever.
Amen.

Small Groups

God's design for our lives is glorious beyond words. He perfectly made us to live in unity with Him as channels of His love, grace and authority. The more we become one with Christ, the more we will be blessed to share in His joy, pleasure, and pure delight.

Throughout the *One with Christ* series, we explored God's design of love. The Father desperately wants to share His love for Jesus with us. When our hearts burn with the Father's love, it will naturally flow in our relationships to the Spirit of Jesus within other believers. We will speak words of life, love, encouragement, honour, and humility to one another. And we will selflessly give to meet each other's needs. By doing so, we will keep the new command to love one another. So where do we begin? We all know that love flows strongest in the smallest numbers and so we need to start by meeting together in small groups. In our fellowship, we call our smallest groups, *Teams*.

Teams

Teams are groups of between two and four people who are devoted to living in God's design of love. The goal of these groups is to:
- actively spur each other on to love, which involves:
    - being accountable to the commands of love
    - encouraging each other to greater depths of intimacy and unity with Jesus
    - praying for healing and empowerment through the Spirit and investing in each other's lives
- live in the light with one another, which involves:
    - confessing any sin
    - sharing victories over temptation
    - honestly expressing your heart with one another

The following questions are designed to help people grow in their design of love.[1] You do not need to ask all these questions every time you meet in a team, but instead be free to follow the leading of the Holy Spirit. Everything that is shared in the group should remain in strict confidence.

Have you sinned in the last week?
It is important when confessing sin to each other to show grace to one another, releasing the assurance of forgiveness and the cleansing power of the blood of Jesus to wash away all sin. In most cases, the confession of sin will bring a real sense of freedom and joy.

Have you faced any temptations over the last week? How did you overcome those temptations?
Temptations will often come, and it is important to create an expectation of overcoming in the face of temptation.

Did you do anything in the last week that you were unsure of whether it was righteous or sinful?
This question explores the grey areas in life where the enemy may try to seduce or distract us, or where the Lord may be working.

Is there anything in your life you would rather keep hidden?
The more transparent we become with each other, the more we will experience the joy of being truly known and loved by one another. There is amazing freedom to be found in being transparent with one another, however at first, people may find it difficult to share honestly with others. Living in the light feels vulnerable and requires great humility, so we need to always respond with real grace and love and keep encouraging each other in the pursuit of love.

How did you express the love of God over the last week?
This question helps us to focus on sharing the love of God with others.

Did you miss any opportunities to love over the last week?
This question helps us to be accountable for the opportunities that the Lord gives us to express His love for people.

Did you share God's joy over the last week?
This question reminds us of how Jesus longs to share His great joy with us.

Did you increase your capacity for love over the last week?
This question focuses on taking risks when loving others. It also helps us to view relational challenges (such as betrayal or offense) as opportunities to increase our capacity for love.

Have you been hearing the voice of God over the last week? What has He been saying? Have you obeyed His voice?
This question creates space to share about our own intimacy with Jesus.

If Jesus were here and asked, "What do you want me to do for you?" what would you say?
This question challenges us to share our deepest desires and helps us to truly get to know each other.

Have you been able to think "We" over the last week?
This reminds people to account for the unity they share with Jesus in the way they think. It is a simple and effective way to involve Jesus in everyday life.

Have you met the needs of others over the last week?
This question focuses us on the practical expressions of love.

Do you have any needs?
This gives us the chance to truly love each other by meeting each other's needs.

In what way can we encourage you or help you in your spiritual growth?
This question allows the team to explore the different ways that we can help one another to pursue maturity in Christ.

Fellowship Groups

These groups are like families of faith and can be any size up to 20 people, though 12 is close to ideal. The focus of these groups is on loving one another, fellowship, teaching, worship, encouragement, ministry, and on sharing the gospel. Within the conversations that take place between people in such meetings, we suggest asking questions like the following:

How have you loved others over the last week? Have you found joy in loving others?
These questions invite us to share a testimony of the love of God in our lives.

Have you been delighting in God, in His word, in prayer, and in worship?
This question explores our relationship with God and helps us to focus on finding our joy and delight in Christ.

How has the Lord been speaking to you lately? What has He been saying?
This question creates an expectancy regarding hearing the voice of God.

How are you pursuing your design of love (loving God with all your being, and loving Him through others)?
This question keeps the greatest command in focus.

Have you faced any distractions in the pursuit of love and holiness? How did you overcome those distractions?
This question acknowledges that the enemy will be constantly trying to hinder us from living in our design of love. It also creates the expectation that we will overcome those distractions with the help of God.

Have you faced discouragement or the temptation to isolate this week?
These are two common strategies of the enemy to lead us away from love.

What qualities of Christ's character do you want to grow in?
This question helps us to remember that Jesus always wants to share more of Himself with us.

What do you need?
This is another way of asking, "how can I love you?"

Special Focus Groups

These groups are formed for a specific purpose for a season. They are usually based around a gifting or ministry and can be used to develop maturity in a specific area of spiritual life. For example, the Lord may lead someone in a team or fellowship group to begin a worship group. Those who feel led to participate can then join in. These special focus groups are a key way to help people to grow in their calling. They give people the opportunity to mature by practising using their gifts and expressing their unique love for Jesus.

These groups can be many and varied. The focus of such groups may include:
- helping others to learn how to move in their spiritual gifts
- sharing the gospel with new or non-believers
- praise and worship
- prayer ministry
- missions
- teaching and theology groups
- community ministry groups
- project groups

We would encourage you both to invest deeply in a weekly team meeting and a fellowship group meeting in your area. More resources for small groups can be found online at oneanother.net.

Study Guide

> **1 Timothy 1:5** (NASB)
> But the goal of our instruction is love from a pure heart and a good conscience and a sincere faith.

The goal of this book is to help you experience the love of God that flows through a truly pure heart. I long for you to experience the power of the cross and such unity with the Spirit of Jesus that you would be able to say with complete conviction, "I have been crucified with Christ and it is no longer I who live but Christ who lives in me!"

Being crucified with Christ is one of the most awesome gifts of God. It is the death of our old life that frees us to live the life that God designed for us: a life of wholehearted love, deep intimacy, and joy-filled unity with the Spirit of Jesus! This kind of life is not something we can just learn about and then claim for ourselves. It is only possible as we take a journey of relationship. And for this journey, God has given us a guide.

> **Galatians 5:25**
> If we live by the Spirit, let us also keep in step with the Spirit.

> **John 16:13**
> When the Spirit of truth comes, he will guide you into all the truth [reality], for he will not speak on his own authority, but whatever he hears he will speak, and he will declare to you the things that are to come.

The Holy Spirit is our guide into reality. He is the One who breathes life into the word and makes the truth real for us. When He speaks to us, the Holy Spirit gives us the faith we need to receive His grace and access the promises of God in our lives.

Knowing this, each chapter of the Study Guide contains exercises to help you to connect and bond with the Holy Spirit. These exercises can be used for personal or group study, and you are of course free to write your own questions or use different Scriptures to meditate on.

Reflect

During His time on earth, Jesus often asked people challenging questions. Questions help us to explore our own hearts and discover our own spiritual strengths and weaknesses. Be encouraged to think deeply and honestly about the questions in the "Reflect" sections. The more honest you can be when forming your answers, the more empowered you will be to grow.

Note that the point of this section is always to inspire spiritual growth; it is never to condemn or discourage you. So if you discover a lack or an issue in your heart while thinking through these questions, be thankful! God is revealing your lack in order to meet your need, to set you free, and to lead you into maturity. With this goal in mind, please be encouraged to take your insights from these questions and process them with Jesus.

Write

Psalm 139:17
How precious to me are your thoughts, O God!
How vast is the sum of them!

In Chapters 11-12 of *First Love,* we look at how God delights to share His thoughts with us. Communication is the key to intimacy, so as we learn to discern the thoughts of God, our intimacy with Jesus will naturally grow.

With intimacy as our goal, in the "Write" section, we take a pen and paper and ask God a question. We then ask the Holy Spirit to share the thoughts of God with us in response and we write down the thoughts that come to mind.

Note that it is possible to mishear God or confuse our own thoughts with His, so after you have finished, it is important to test what you have written. In Chapter 13 of *First Love*, we learn how to test the thoughts we receive by comparing them to the word of God, the witness of the Spirit, and the sense of life in the thought. We also learn to test them against the standard of love by asking: Do these thoughts lead to a greater love for God and a selfless love for others? If so, we can treasure them as a precious gift from God.

Imagine

> Joshua 1:8
>
> This Book of the Law shall not depart from your mouth, but you shall meditate on it day and night, so that you may be careful to do according to all that is written in it. For then you will make your way prosperous, and then you will have good success.

Scripture calls us to constantly meditate on the truth. Biblical meditation is not the emptying of the mind but the filling of both our hearts and minds with the word of God. An essential part of this kind of mediation is learning to use our imagination. Many people are hesitant to do this because the world so often uses imagination to indulge in fantasies. However, God created our imagination to be used in a positive way to bring spiritual transformation. In Chapter One of *First Love,* we learn how God uses our imagination to impress His word on our heart and change us from within.

In the "Imagine" section, we ask God to inspire our imagination and help us to picture the truth of God as if it was real in our lives. As we do this, we create space for the Spirit of God to speak to us and turn our faith into vision. God can then use our vision to lead us into transformation.

1. Seek First the Kingdom

Please read the Study Guide introduction before beginning.

Reflect

Is there any instinct within me to try and earn anything from God?

Am I truly seeking the will of God?

What does it mean to give up my right to govern my own life?

Do I have faith like a child when it comes to the call of wholehearted love?

Write

Lord, are there any areas in my heart where I am not letting you reign?

Imagine

> **Mark 10:14**
> But when Jesus saw it, he was indignant and said to them, "Let the children come to me; do not hinder them, for to such belongs the kingdom of God. Truly, I say to you, whoever does not receive the kingdom of God like a child shall not enter it."

Imagine being like a child and hearing Jesus share His thoughts with you. Imagine Him calling you to love Him with your entire being. Would you doubt Him? Or would you listen in awe? Imagine Jesus opening your eyes to see His vision for your life.

2. Kingdom Within

Reflect

Who is really in possession of my life right now?

How can I be sure that God will provide all my needs?

Is there any area in my life where I can depend more upon God?

Do I feel free to selflessly love others?

Write

Lord, who do you want to love through me today? How?

Imagine

> Matthew 6:31-33
> "Therefore do not be anxious, saying, 'What shall we eat?' or 'What shall we drink?' or 'What shall we wear?' For the Gentiles seek after all these things, and your heavenly Father knows that you need them all. But seek first the kingdom of God and his righteousness, and all these things will be added to you."

Imagine Jesus promising to always provide your every need. Imagine living without any stress. Imagine how life would look if the love of God was flowing through every area of your life. Imagine the joy of selfless love.

3. Covenant of Blood

Reflect

Is it possible for God to break His own covenant?

Am I striving in my own strength or sharing the strength of Christ?

What would it look like for Jesus to bear the burden of my obedience?

What does it mean for me to be "in Christ"?

Write

Lord, are you really offering to help me to obey you?

Imagine

> **Genesis 15:17** (NKJV)
> When the sun had gone down and it was dark, behold, a smoking fire pot and a flaming torch passed between these pieces.

Abram was asleep when the smoking firepot and blazing torch passed between the pieces. Imagine watching this happen. How would you feel seeing Jesus make a covenant with the Father on your behalf?

4. For Jesus

Reflect

Do I really believe that God created me as a living expression of His love and goodness?

What has my debt cost Jesus?

Can I imagine myself existing entirely in love and holiness?

What would it feel like for the Father's love for Jesus to flow through me?

Write

Father, how much do you want to love Jesus through me?

Imagine

> **John 17:25-26 (NASB)**
> "O righteous Father, although the world has not known You, yet I have known You; and these have known that You sent Me; and I have made Your name known to them, and will make it known, so that the love with which You loved Me may be in them, and I in them."

Imagine Jesus praying this prayer, just for you. *Father! Let your love for me live in _____ and I in him/her!* Imagine the Spirit of Jesus opening your heart to be filled with the Father's love for Jesus. Imagine His love flowing through every part of your being. Imagine Jesus loving the Father with all His heart through you. Imagine feeling truly alive.

5. The Exchange

Reflect

Do I feel completely innocent before God?

Am I able to fully forget my past sinfulness so it no longer shapes my future?

What would it feel like to share the holiness of Christ?

What does it mean for me to drink the blood of Jesus?

Write

Jesus, what would you like to exchange with me today?

Imagine

> **Hebrews 10:16-17**
> "This is the covenant that I will make with them after those days, says the Lord: I will put my laws upon their heart, and on their mind I will write them," He then says, "and their sins and their lawless deeds I will remember no more."

Take a minute to memorise this verse. Imagine hearing Jesus say to you, "I will make a covenant with you and write my law of love upon your heart and your mind. I will forget all your sins forever. You are clean and innocent in my eyes, and I love you."

6. Eternal Life

Reflect

Is it possible to know Jesus and not to love Him?

How intimately does God want me to know Him?

How much do I want to know God?

How can I increase my devotion to God and so know Him more?

Write

Father, is there anything in my life that is hindering my knowledge of you?

Imagine

> 1 Timothy 6:12
> Fight the good fight of the faith. Take hold of the eternal life to which you were called and about which you made the good confession in the presence of many witnesses.

Imagine Jesus holding your shoulders, staring you in the eyes and speaking these words to you: *"Fight the good fight of the faith. Take hold of eternal life."* How will you respond to Him?

7. Stages of Covenant

Reflect

Why is covenant so important to God?

What does it mean to live in unity with God?

What does it mean for Jesus to circumcise our hearts?

What does our spiritual circumcision achieve?

Write

Father, what is my next step towards my design of love?

Imagine

Ezekiel 36:26-27

"And I will give you a new heart, and a new spirit I will put within you. And I will remove the heart of stone from your flesh and give you a heart of flesh. And I will put my Spirit within you, and cause you to walk in my statutes and be careful to obey my rules."

Take some time to meditate on this verse. Imagine receiving a new heart and being filled afresh with God's Spirit.

Imagine Jesus coming to you and saying, "_____, choose to love me with your entire being and I promise: I will make it possible. I'll give you a new heart and I'll put my Spirit within you. I'll do whatever it takes to empower you to walk in my ways of selfless love. Just say 'Yes' and I will restore your design of love and unity with Me."

8. The Flesh

Reflect

Have I been struggling with any sinful instincts?

Do I think of the flesh nature as a part of me or as a cancer within me?

Is God opposed to my flesh nature?

Do I want God to diagnose me and expose my sinful instincts?

Write

Jesus, what is an area of my life where my selfish nature has been trying to steal, kill or destroy?

Imagine

Psalm 139:23-24
Search me, O God, and know my heart!
 Try me and know my thoughts!
And see if there be any grievous way in me,
 and lead me in the way everlasting!

Psalm 90:8
You have set our iniquities before you,
 our secret sins in the light of your presence.

Imagine coming to Jesus as a patient for a spiritual health check. *Scan me. Examine my heart and mind. Reveal my iniquity, my secret sins, reveal any grievous way in me. And lead me in the way of eternal life into my design of love.*

    Would Jesus show you your scan results or would He hide the truth from you? Would He condemn you for having the cancer of selfishness and sin? Or would He show compassion? Does He really want to save your life?

9. Identity

Reflect

Have I been living in a mixture of Spirit and flesh?

How can I separate spirit and flesh within me?

What would it be like to partake of the divine nature of Christ?

What would it feel like to have love as my primary instinct?

Write

Father, how do you see the real me today?

Imagine

> **John 6:53-55**
> So Jesus said to them, "Truly, truly, I say to you, unless you eat the flesh of the Son of Man and drink his blood, you have no life in you. Whoever feeds on my flesh and drinks my blood has eternal life, and I will raise him up on the last day. For my flesh is true food, and my blood is true drink."

Over the next few weeks, ask the Holy Spirit to prompt you to exchange your flesh with Jesus and partake of His nature. Take some time to pray and meditate on the nature of Christ and allow yourself to be consumed by His love.

10. Circumcising the Heart

Reflect

Does the enemy have anything in me?

Do I really believe that God can remove the selfish nature from my heart?

Do I believe that He wants to?

How can I be crucified with Christ?

Write

Lord, is your promise of a circumcised heart for me?

Imagine

> **John 8:34-36**
> Jesus answered them, "Truly, truly, I say to you, everyone who practices sin is a slave to sin. The slave does not remain in the house forever; the son remains forever. So if the Son sets you free, you will be free indeed."

Imagine hearing Jesus say these words. Imagine His conviction, authority, compassion, and confidence. How free does Jesus want to make you? How able is He to set you free? Imagine Him asking you: "Do you want to be free?"

11. No Other Saviour

Reflect

What risk is there in believing in the circumcision of the heart?

What risk is there in not believing?

Is it possible to have a partially circumcised heart?

Could there be any reason God would leave us with the sinful nature?

Write

Father, is there anything in me that is resisting your design of wholehearted love?

Imagine

> 2 Corinthians 5:14-15 (NKJV)
> For the love of Christ compels us, because we judge thus: that if One died for all, then all died; and He died for all, that those who live should live no longer for themselves, but for Him who died for them and rose again.

Imagine dying with Christ. Imagine your selfish nature being removed from your heart so that you no longer want to live for yourself. Imagine the love of Christ filling you and compelling you. What would that feel like?

12. Everything Already

Reflect

In my own experience, did Jesus remove my sinful nature with all its selfish instincts when I first started following Him?

What is one gift of my inheritance that I have possessed?

What is a gift that I would like to possess?

Would I like to experience the reality of a circumcised heart of love?

Write

Holy Spirit, what gift are you giving me in this season?

Imagine

> **James 1:17**
> Every good gift and every perfect gift is from above, coming down from the Father of lights, with whom there is no variation or shadow due to change.

Imagine Jesus offering you the gift you wrote about above. Imagine holding the box and reading the label. Do you want to unwrap it?

13. Waves Rise Up

Reflect

Have I come to the end of myself?

Are there any areas in my life where I am agreeing with my flesh nature?

If the Father asked me how much I love Jesus, what would my response be right now?

What do I want my response to be?

Write

Father, is now my time for the circumcision of the heart, or are you calling me to focus on something else?

Imagine

> **Luke 8: 23-24**
> And a windstorm came down on the lake, and they were filling with water and were in danger. And they went and woke him, saying, "Master, Master, we are perishing!" And he awoke and rebuked the wind and the raging waves, and they ceased, and there was a calm.

Imagine being in the boat with Jesus. Imagine being caught in a great storm and truly believing that you are going to die. Are you ready to cry out to Him?

14. Not I but Christ

Reflect

Have I been trusting in my physical death to set me free from my sinful nature?

Have I had enough of sin?

What does "no longer I" really mean to me?

What does it mean for Jesus to live in me?

Write

Father, what is the next step for me towards the cross and wholehearted love?

Imagine

> **Galatians 2:20**
> I have been crucified with Christ. It is no longer I who live, but Christ who lives in me. And the life I now live in the flesh [body] I live by faith in the Son of God, who loved me and gave himself for me.

Imagine Jesus calling you saying, "Come and be crucified with Me! I will take you into death and it will be no longer you, but I who live in you." Come, take up your cross and follow Me." What is your response?

15. Set Apart

Reflect

What does it mean to be created in the image of God?

Why would Satan fight so hard to keep us from being crucified with Christ?

Is wholehearted love worth fighting for?

Do I want to remain a slave to sin for my whole life?

Write

Jesus, how can I embrace the cross and be fully united with you in death and life?

Imagine

> **1 Thessalonians 5:23-24**
> Now may the God of peace himself sanctify you completely, and may your whole spirit and soul and body be kept blameless at the coming of our Lord Jesus Christ. He who calls you is faithful; he will surely do it.

Take some time to memorise this verse. Imagine the power of the blood of Jesus flowing into you and sanctifying you *completely*. What would it feel like for Jesus to remove your selfish nature? What would it feel like for your entire heart to be filled with His peace and love? Faithful is He who calls you, He surely will do it.

16. Righteous Judgment

Reflect

Am I confident that God is never angry with the real me?

Do I like the idea that God's wrath is directed towards my flesh nature?

Is there anything in me that would fear God's judgment?

Am I willing to ask God to judge me?

Write

Jesus, are you calling me to drink from your cup?

Imagine

> **1 Corinthians 15:55-57**
> "O death, where is your victory?
> O death, where is your sting?"
>
> The sting of death is sin, and the power of sin is the law. But thanks be to God, who gives us the victory through our Lord Jesus Christ.

Imagine the joy that Jesus felt after He had finished drinking the cup that the Father had given Him, knowing that death had lost its sting forever. Imagine the joy He feels when His children willingly drink of His cup.

17. Immersed in Fire

Reflect

Am I separating the sinful nature from my identity?

Do I want my sin nature to be judged and consumed?

What would it feel like to be saturated in the consuming love of Jesus?

Write

Loving God, how would you like to flow your love to me today?

Imagine

Revelation 1:12-16

Then I turned to see the voice that was speaking to me, and on turning I saw seven golden lampstands, and in the midst of the lampstands one like a son of man, clothed with a long robe and with a golden sash around his chest. The hairs of his head were white, like white wool, like snow. His eyes were like a flame of fire, his feet were like burnished bronze, refined in a furnace, and his voice was like the roar of many waters. In his right hand he held seven stars, from his mouth came a sharp two-edged sword, and his face was like the sun shining in full strength.

Imagine Jesus looking at you with eyes of blazing fire. Imagine that fire consuming you. What would it feel like to have His fire burning within you?

18. Judgment and Design

Reflect

Do I believe that I need other people in my life?

Do I believe that others need me?

Am I willing to love Jesus in His people by meeting their needs?

Am I confident about my eternal judgment?

Write

Father, who do you want to love through me today? Is there a need in someone's life that we can meet together today?

Father, are there some people that I can regularly connect with and start to love by meeting their needs? If so, who?

Imagine

> **Matthew 25:34**
> "Then the King will say to those on his right, 'Come, you who are blessed by my Father, inherit the kingdom prepared for you from the foundation of the world.'"

Imagine the Day of Judgment. Imagine the joy of standing before the Father and hearing Him say, "Well done. You loved my Son well. Come inherit My Kingdom."

Act

Contact some of the people that God has put on your heart to meet with.

19. Renewing the Mind

Reflect

Can I recognise any strongholds of lies that have been built in my mind?

Is there a stronghold of truth that Jesus wants to build in me?

Is there any area in my life that I need to start thinking "We"?

What difference would thinking "We" make to that area?

Write

Lord, you say that the weapons of our warfare have divine power to destroy strongholds. What is one stronghold that you would like to destroy or one that you would like to build in me today?

Imagine

> **2 Corinthians 10:4**
> For the weapons of our warfare are not of the flesh but have divine power to destroy strongholds.

Imagine seeing an ungodly fortress in your mind. Imagine looking at the stones at its foundation and reading the lies. Imagine smashing those stones and seeing the fortress tremble and start to fall.

> **Isaiah 54:11-12 (NASB)**
> "O afflicted one, storm-tossed, and not comforted,
>   Behold, I will set your stones in antimony,
>   And your foundations I will lay in sapphires.
> "Moreover, I will make your battlements of rubies,
>   And your gates of crystal,
>   And your entire wall of precious stones."

Now imagine building a stronghold with the Lord. Imagine Him placing precious stones at its foundation, each representing a truth. Imagine the beauty of your mind increasing as the stronghold is built.

20. Blessing or Curse?

Reflect

Do I believe that my life is connected to the generations before me?

Are there any negative patterns in my family line, such as divorce, addiction, depression, anxiety, poverty, rage, lust, failure and so on?

Are there any positive patterns in my family line, such as joyful marriages, loyalty, humility, prosperity, success, respect and so on?

Imagine

Colossians 2:13-15
And you, who were dead in your trespasses and the uncircumcision of your flesh, God made alive together with him, having forgiven us all our trespasses, by cancelling the record of debt that stood against us with its legal demands. This he set aside, nailing it to the cross. He disarmed the rulers and authorities and put them to open shame, by triumphing over them in him.

Imagine the enemy being stripped of his legal right to afflict your bloodlines through generational iniquity. Imagine him being totally disarmed. Imagine the victory in seeing every curse exchanged for a blessing over your family line for generations to come.

21. The Fight of Faith

Reflect

Do I really believe that Jesus lives in me?

What strategies has the enemy been using against me?

Do I have soldiers who are fighting with me?

Do they know my vulnerabilities?

Write

Father, am I agreeing with any lies of the enemy right now?

Imagine

1 Corinthians 10:13

No temptation has overtaken you that is not common to man. God is faithful, and he will not let you be tempted beyond your ability, but with the temptation he will also provide the way of escape, that you may be able to endure it.

Romans 8:33-37

Who will bring a charge against God's elect? God is the one who justifies; who is the one who condemns? Christ Jesus is He who died, yes, rather who was raised, who is at the right hand of God, who also intercedes for us. Who will separate us from the love of Christ? Will tribulation, or distress, or persecution, or famine, or nakedness, or peril, or sword? Just as it is written,

"For Your sake we are being put to death all day long;
We were considered as sheep to be slaughtered."

But in all these things we overwhelmingly conquer through Him who loved us.

Imagine Jesus leading you onto the battlefield. Imagine Jesus showing you the enemy's strategies in advance, revealing how you can escape and how you can stand and overcome. Then imagine Him clothing you with the armour of light and filling you with His presence. Imagine the Spirit of Jesus within you wielding the sword of truth and lifting the shield of faith in perfect unity with you. Imagine overwhelming victory.

22. All Authority

Reflect

How can I know if a demon is oppressing someone?

How can I tell if a person is acting in their flesh or acting under the influence of a demon?

Have I been pandering to the selfish nature in people around me?

How can I relate to people for who they truly are?

Write

Father, what steps can we take to building a greater awareness of the spiritual realm?

Imagine

> **1 John 5:4**
> For everyone who has been born of God overcomes the world. And this is the victory that has overcome the world—our faith.

> **Revelation 12:10-11**
> And I heard a loud voice in heaven, saying, "Now the salvation and the power and the kingdom of our God and the authority of his Christ have come, for the accuser of our brothers has been thrown down, who accuses them day and night before our God. And they have conquered him by the blood of the Lamb and by the word of their testimony, for they loved not their lives even unto death."

Imagine Jesus sharing His faith with you. Imagine feeling the confidence of Christ filling your heart and mind. Imagine this faith empowering you to experience new realms of love and to bring you victory in every battle. Imagine overcoming the enemy through the blood of the Lamb and the word of your testimony. Take some time to proclaim the authority, power and glory of God.

23. Overpowering Principalities

Reflect

Am I in a team of two or three people who are real with each other and meet to encourage one another?

Am I obeying the call to love?

What would it look like to join with others to possess the spiritual gates of my community?

What would it look like to weave others into the body of Christ?

Write

Father, how can I grow in your authority?

Imagine
> Isaiah 9:6-7
> For to us a child is born,
> > to us a son is given;
> > and the government shall be upon his shoulder,
> > and his name shall be called
> Wonderful Counsellor, Mighty God,
> > Everlasting Father, Prince of Peace.
> Of the increase of his government and of peace
> > there will be no end,
> > on the throne of David and over his kingdom,
> > to establish it and to uphold it
> > with justice and with righteousness
> > from this time forth and forevermore.
> The zeal of the Lord of hosts will do this.

Imagine Jesus taking the full weight of government in your life, releasing His peace, justice and righteousness into your life. Imagine connecting with a few other believers and releasing His authority in your community. Imagine seeing people set free to receive the love of God. Imagine God's kingdom coming and His will being done in your community as it is in heaven.

24. Journey of Love

Reflect

What did the Torah teach Israel about their design?

What spiritual parallels can I see between my life and the journey of Israel?

Where am I in the journey?

Why did the people refuse the blessing of the Land?

Write

Lord, what is one lesson I can learn from Israel's journey to the Promised Land?

Imagine

> **1 Corinthians 2:9-10 (NASB)**
> But just as it is written,
>
>> "Things which eye has not seen and ear has not heard,
>> And which have not entered the heart of man,
>> All that God has prepared for those who love Him."
>
> For to us God revealed them through the Spirit; for the Spirit searches all things, even the depths of God.

Imagine the kind of inheritance that God has prepared for you. Imagine a life better than anything you could hope to ask for—a life saturated in divine love and filled with His presence. Imagine standing at the edge of your Promised Land, knowing that you will have to fight for this life. Imagine being at the edge of the Jordan. How are you feeling in your heart?

25. Into the Land

Reflect

What parts of my journey have I already experienced?

Have I truly left my old life?

Am I living life as a desert wanderer or a land conqueror?

Am I like the Shulamite, leaning on my Beloved?

Write

Jesus, where am I in my journey towards my Promised Land?

Imagine

> **Song of Solomon 4:11**
> "Your lips drip nectar, my bride; honey and milk are under your tongue; the fragrance of your garments is like the fragrance of Lebanon."

The Promised Land flows with milk and honey. Imagine that Jesus is your Promised Land and you are His. Imagine Him enjoying milk and honey with every word you speak to Him. Imagine a life of abundant love, intimacy and joy with Jesus, the Lover of your soul.

26. Choose Life

Reflect

Have I chosen life by choosing a life of selfless love, intimacy and unity with God?

Are my works flowing to God or from God?

Have I found rest for my soul?

Is it more important for me to be blessed or to be a blessing?

Write

Father, is there any area where I am trying to mix selfishness with my spiritual life? Or is there any area where my heart has become hardened?

Imagine

> Matthew 6:25, 33-34 (NKJV)
> "Therefore I say to you, do not worry about your life, what you will eat or what you will drink; nor about your body, what you will put on. Is not life more than food and the body more than clothing?
> "...But seek first the kingdom of God and His righteousness, and all these things shall be added to you. Therefore do not worry about tomorrow, for tomorrow will worry about its own things. Sufficient for the day is its own trouble."

Imagine Jesus speaking these words to you. Imagine Jesus offering His yoke to you and promising rest. Imagine putting His yoke on and feeling all stress leave you *forever*. Imagine a life free from stress and striving, working with Jesus as a channel of His love.

About the Author

My name is Geoff (pronounced "Jeff"), and I am an author, speaker, and founder of the Freeslaves.org project. I live in Dunedin, New Zealand, with my wife Melanie and our four children.

I started following Jesus as a child, but it was not until my early twenties that I began to come out of legalism and into the grace of His awe-inspiring love. I now live to love Jesus. He has done more in my life than I could ever express, and I pray He will always be my reason, my passion, my vision, and my goal.

Jesus says that Scripture depends on the commands to love God and love others. In the *One with Christ* series of books, I do my best to interpret the Scriptures through this lens of love in dependence on the Holy Spirit. If I have fallen short of this in any way, I ask you for your grace to look past any imperfections and to see the goal of the book, which is to help you to:

- Make a covenant with God to love Him with all your heart, soul, mind and strength,
- Experience the power of the cross to circumcise your heart,
- To live out your life in God's design of love, intimacy, and unity with Jesus

If you would like to learn more, ask a question, share a testimony, or connect with me, please visit onewithchrist.org.

All blessings and love in Christ,

Reference Notes

Introduction
[1] Philippians 2:13
[2] See John 6:60, 66

1. Seek First the Kingdom
[1] Note that this does not mean that we can earn our way into relationship with God. Every dimension of relationship is a gift of grace that we can only receive by faith, but the same faith that enables us to receive God's grace also compels us to change. We can see this in the natural realm. When we get married, we know that our husband or wife is sharing their lives with us as a free gift. But we also accept that we need to devote our lives exclusively to them in order to fully receive the gift. This does not undermine grace in any way. Rather, it simply means that to fully experience a relationship, we need to make changes on our part.

2. Kingdom Within
[1] Acts 19:11-17
[2] Quoted from *Rees Howells: Intercessor, 2001 Lutterworth Press.*
[3] Acts 4:32
[4] 1 Timothy 6:7

3. Covenant of Blood
[1] Deuteronomy 4:24, Deuteronomy 9:3, Hebrews 12:29
[2] Isaiah 62:1
[3] Luke 2:25-32
[4] Ephesians 1:3-4

4. For Jesus
[1] Hebrews 13:20-21
[2] In *Bride Arise*, I talk briefly about how the Lord prompted us to start the freeslaves.org project. This project beautifully illustrates the principles of

redemption and forgiveness. In many parts of the world, people become trapped in bonded-labour slavery when they desperately need money, most often people to pay for the medical costs of a family member. They take a loan from a business such as a brick-kiln or quarry and sign a contract to live and work at the business until they pay back the loan. However, they soon learn that because the interest rate on the loan is so high and their pay is so low, they are unable to repay the loan. This leaves them trapped forever in a life of exploitation and abuse.

For these families, their debt is their ransom. We redeem the people by paying the debt they owe their enslavers and then forgive the debt they owe us. Why? Because Jesus did exactly the same thing for us at the cross. He redeemed us from the enemy, cancelling all rights the enemy had to enslave us, and He forgave our debt, setting us free.

If you would like to know what it feels like to redeem an enslaved person, please visit freeslaves.org

[3] Ephesians 1:3

[4] Romans 1:17, Galatians 3:11

5. The Exchange

[1] Justify (*dikaioo*) is derived from the word *dikaios*, meaning righteous.

[2] See Hebrews 8:6-12, Jeremiah 31:31-34

[3] As we confess our sin, the blood of Jesus washes away our sin and we are made entirely innocent before God (1 John 1:9). In the Spirit, we are clean and pure. It really is as if we never sinned. Being forgiven and washed clean does not always mean that we will avoid the natural consequences of sin. People may still be hurt and restoration may still be required. However, being cleansed by the blood does mean that we are set free from the spiritual consequences of sin. Our sin is washed away and the separation and spiritual death that our sin creates are gone forever. God no longer remembers the sin and neither should we. Like Paul, we should forget what is behind us and focus on our future in Christ (Philippians 3:13, Luke 9:62).

[4] Note the close relationship between the Greek words sanctify (*hagiazo*) and purify (*hagnizo*), both of which share the root word *hagios*, meaning holy. This word is defined by HELPS Word-studies as follows:

> *hágios*: properly, different (unlike), other ("otherness"), holy; for the believer, hágios means "likeness of nature with the Lord" because "different from the

world." The fundamental (core) meaning of hágios is "different" – thus a temple in the 1st century was hagios ("holy") because different from other buildings (Wm. Barclay). In the NT, hágios ("holy") has the "technical" meaning "different from the world" because "like the Lord."

(© 1987, 2011 by Helps Ministries, Inc.)

Thus being made holy through sanctification produces a tangible change in our hearts and minds. We become different from the world and different from our former life. We are different because we are united with Jesus in the likeness of His nature and love.

5 In some translations the Greek word *oxos* is translated as vinegar rather than sour wine. Vinegar essentially is sour wine. It may be of interest to note that the English word vinegar comes from the French *vin aigre*, literally meaning sour or tart wine.

6 2 Timothy 2:25: True repentance is a gift of God.

7 See Hebrews 12:10 for sharing the holiness of Christ.

8 John 6:53

6. Eternal Life

1 It is important to note that *eis* can change its meaning and nuance in different contexts. In John 3:16 and other places, it is not necessarily incorrect to translate *eis* with the word *in*, but by doing so the text loses the underlying sense of unity contained in the word *eis*.

2 Mark 13:28

3 1 Timothy 1:5

4 See Genesis 4:1, 17, 25; 19:8; 24:16; Numbers 31:17-18, 35; Judges 11:39; 19:25; 21:12; 1 Samuel 1:19; 1 Kings 1:4; Matthew 1:25.

5 Jesus is speaking in a passage that starts at John 13 and finishes at the end of John 17. When we study these chapters as a whole, we can clearly see the central themes of love and unity. For evidence of these themes see: John 13:34, John 14:10, 15, 16, 20, 21, 23; John 15:4, 5, 7, 10, 12, 17; John 16:27; John 17:11, 20-26. The key message Jesus is sharing is one of being united to God in love.

> **Love** (quotes from John 13-17)
> A new commandment I give to you, that you love one another: just as I have loved you, you also are to love one another. If you love me, you will keep my commandments. In that day you will know that I am in my

Father, and you in me, and I in you. And he who loves me will be loved by my Father, and I will love him and manifest myself to him. If anyone loves me, he will keep my word, and my Father will love him, and we will come to him and make our home with him. The Father himself loves you, because you have loved me and have believed that I came from God. If you keep my commandments, you will abide in my love, just as I have kept my Father's commandments and abide in his love. This is my commandment, that you love one another as I have loved you. These things I command you, so that you will love one another. O righteous Father, I made known to them your name, and I will continue to make it known, that the love with which you have loved me may be in them, and I in them.

Unity (quotes from John 13-17)
Do you not believe that I am in the Father and the Father is in me? The Father who dwells in me does his works. Abide in me, and I in you. Whoever abides in me and I in him, he it is that bears much fruit. If you abide in me, and my words abide in you, ask whatever you wish, and it will be done for you.

Holy Father, keep them in your name, which you have given me, that they may be one, even as we are one…that they may all be one, just as you, Father, are in me, and I in you, that they also may be in us, so that the world may believe that you have sent me. The glory that you have given me I have given to them, that they may be one even as we are one, I in them and you in me, that they may become perfectly one, so that the world may know that you sent me and loved them even as you loved me.

[6] We can see the connection between devotion and intimacy at work in every type of relationship. The depth of our natural relationships is almost always determined by an unspoken but agreed level of commitment and vulnerability. In the early stages of a relationship we typically look for common ground. If a person shows little interest in us, then we are naturally more guarded in what we share. We secure our hearts and relate to the other person on their level. In simple terms, we meet people where they are at and develop a relationship from there. God does the same with us.

⁷ This may be one of the reasons why divorce rates are higher for people who have had multiple sexual partners before marriage.

7. Stages of Covenant

¹ The first outworking of this command is the second most important command: to love our neighbours as ourselves.

² Visit www.onewithchrist.org for more on types. The Passover lamb is a type of Jesus as our sacrificial lamb (1 Corinthians 5:7); the rock in the wilderness is a type of Jesus, who is the Rock of our Salvation (1 Corinthians 10:1-4); Adam, Moses, David, and Solomon are all types of Jesus (Romans 5:14-17, Acts 3:17-22, Daniel 4:3, Matthew 27:37, Matthew 21:9).

³ See Galatians 5:1-3. Also note that in 1 Corinthians 7:18-19, Paul expressly writes that people who are uncircumcised in their flesh should not circumcise themselves. It is the heart alone that matters.

⁴ See Deuteronomy 10:12-22, Jeremiah 4:3-4, Jeremiah 9:25-26, Ezekiel 44:4-9, Acts 7:51-53, Mark 7:14-23

8. The Flesh

¹ There are different perspectives on what the "flesh" is exactly. Some people believe that it refers to self-generated actions that we do apart from faith. Others think of it as the human personality as created by God but corrupted by sin. Others think of the *flesh* in terms of a mindset or identity. They say that those who live according to the flesh have a distorted view of their own identity. Yet, if the flesh was simply a corruption of something that God created such as the human nature or mind, then Scripture would call for a renewing of the flesh so it could be restored back to God's intended design. This is never the case—not even once. Scripture never calls for the redemption of the flesh but only its destruction.

Therefore, because the enemy sowed sin and selfishness into the hearts of people, we do not consider the flesh to be merely a corruption of the mind or personality—something that can be healed and renewed. For the purposes of this book, we speak of the *flesh* as the nature of sin within us that produces sinful instincts and desires, and we consider it something that can be overcome and removed from our lives through the cross.

² For example, See CEV and NLT translations in Galatians 5:24.

³ See 1 Corinthians 13:1-3. When we choose selfishness over love, we make ourselves *nothing*.

[4] Note that the enemy knows that emotions of love are often passionate, intense and addictive. So to preserve selfishness, the enemy distorts sexual love to accommodate selfishness, presenting passion as only existing within the domain of lust. Because of the power lust to gratify the old self, the world encourages the pursuit of an emotional, lustful experience of sexual affection, and it belittles love without such self-gratifying passion. This is a corrupt distortion of a pure reality. Lust is not love. Why? Because the very nature of love is selfless. Love edifies rather than gratifies. Love always gives whereas lust always takes. Love serves rather than dominates. The flesh or old self finds nothing but the threat of death in true love, which is why it would attempt to distract us with lust. When the flesh nature sees the love of God approaching, it compels us to run from love as it prepares to fight for its life. We must all be prepared to fight our fallen instincts and run to Love.

[5] See 1 John 3:14-15

[6] Colossians 2:20-23

9. Identity

[1] John 4:24

[2] Ezekiel 36:22-28

10. Circumcising the Heart

[1] 1 John 3:13-4

[2] Deuteronomy 30:6

[3] Luke 10:25-28

[4] Matthew 3:1-10

[5] See Ephesians 4:24, Genesis 1:26

[6] Romans 13:14

11. No Other Saviour

[1] 1 Timothy 4:1, Matthew 15:9

[2] In *Bride Arise*, we saw how bringing a person to devote their lives to loving God with all their heart is what it means to prepare the bride for Jesus. Imagine being a teacher and finally appearing before the Father. Imagine hearing Him say, "I called you to prepare a bride for My Son. Where is she?" The Father's love for Jesus is why teachers will be held to a stricter judgment. We must align all our teaching towards preparing people as a bride for Jesus by calling her into her design of love.

[3] 1 Corinthians 15:54-57

4. *Entire Sanctification – Adam Clarke*
5. By teaching that we cannot be free from sin until physical death, this doctrine rejects the power of the blood of Jesus to completely deliver people from sin. To say that the blood of Jesus is insufficient is profoundly dishonouring to Christ's sacrifice at the cross. Scripture is emphatic on this point: Jesus' blood cleanses us from all sin (1 John 1:7-10). The power of the blood is absolute. A single drop of the blood of Christ would have enough power to purge all humanity of our indwelling sin. And yet His blood poured from His side. The cross is more than enough to cleanse us from all sin. No other deliverance is necessary and nothing but faith is needed to access the power of Jesus' blood to wash away all our sin.
6. Scripture makes it clear that Jesus died for forgiveness *and* deliverance. At the cross, He did not just forgive the effects of our sin, but He took away sin itself. In order to honour His sacrifice, we must enter into the full power of the cross and then share it with others.
7. This teaching implies that Christ did not fully pay our debt nor bear the full judgment of God upon sin. For if indwelling sin only leaves us when we physically die, then we are forced to bear a judgment upon sin apart from Christ. This belief echoes the Roman Catholic belief in purgatory. This teaching about purgatory states that when we physically die we enter a purifying process that makes us holy so we can gain entry into heaven. Any form of this teaching is entirely opposed to the cross. The cross is God's only solution for sin. There is no other way to be purified but through faith in the blood of Jesus.
8. Believing that the selfish nature only dies completely when we physically die presumes that sin is inherently physical rather than spiritual. Yet Scripture describes the sinful nature as a spiritual condition which requires a spiritual death through faith rather than a physical death (see Chapter Five). God created our physical bodies and He did not make them sinful.
9. God did not create us with the sin nature, nor did He design us for selfishness. The selfish nature was sown by Satan in the Garden. By suggesting that Jesus' death was insufficient to remove the selfish nature, this teaching implies that the work of Satan was greater than the work of Christ. In other words, Jesus failed at the cross. He came intending to break the curse of sin and death by removing the selfish nature, but His blood was not enough. It seems that Adam's sin created a selfishness that was too deeply engrained in humanity for the blood of Jesus to conquer.

Romans 5:15-17 (NLT, emphasis added)

But there is a great difference between Adam's sin and God's gracious gift. For the sin of this one man, Adam, brought death to many. But **even greater** is God's wonderful grace and his gift of forgiveness to many through this other man, Jesus Christ. And the result of God's gracious gift is very different from the result of that one man's sin. For Adam's sin led to condemnation, but God's free gift leads to our being made right with God, even though we are guilty of many sins. For the sin of this one man, Adam, caused death to rule over many. But **even greater** is God's wonderful grace and his gift of righteousness, for all who receive it will live in triumph over sin and death through this one man, Jesus Christ.

The cross is far greater than Adam's fall. The sacrifice of Christ was more than sufficient to overcome sin. It is the greater force in every way, bringing life and righteousness to us through our unity with Jesus Christ. Jesus won and Satan lost.

[10] See 1 John 3:8. Jesus came to destroy the works of the devil. And so what are those works? The greatest work the enemy ever did was to sow the sinful nature into the hearts of God's creation. Jesus came to destroy the works of the enemy and He did not fail. The cross was enough to completely destroy the nature that the enemy sowed in our hearts.

[11] See Galatians 3:10-13. Jesus redeemed us from the curse of sin by becoming a curse. He was crowned with thorns, which represent the curse. What more could He have done to break the curse? The reality is that Jesus became a curse for us to fully break every curse over us, including the curse of sin and death. The cross was enough!

[12] Teaching that we are only free from sin when we physically die denies all the Scriptures that speak of the old self being killed, crucified, circumcised, removed, and put to death in this life.

In order to believe that physical death destroys the selfish nature and still believe the Bible, people often teach that the death of the flesh is an ongoing, daily experience which is ended only in physical death. Yet by definition, death is an event that happens at the point in time when life ends. Death is death, not a constant state of dying. By negating the sense of completion in death, this teaching challenges the integrity and trustworthiness of Scripture. Scripture uses the word *death* rather than *dying* because that is exactly what the cross does to the selfish nature. It kills it. Completely.

[13] By saying that the blood of Jesus does not cleanse us from all sin, this doctrine refutes Christ's declaration of victory on the cross: "It is finished!" (John 19:30). Jesus believed that God's work of delivering people from their sin and restoring us to Himself was forever complete and finished. To teach that full deliverance from sin only comes with physical death suggests that the work of the cross was not truly finished and that Jesus was mistaken. Perhaps He should have said, "It is almost finished! Now you just have to physically die and then you'll be free from sin. Who would like to be saved first?"

[14] The selfish nature occupies space in our hearts. This means that it is impossible to love God with all our heart while it still lives within us. If we cannot be set free from the selfish nature in this life, then we are doomed to live in ongoing disobedience to the first command. And it is all God's fault. For when God gave us a command that we could never keep, He condemned us to a life of ongoing sin, rebellion and futility.

This makes absolutely no sense. God is Love. He died to set us free from our sin, not to bind us in it. When God gives us the command of wholehearted love, He gives us His promise that He will make it possible. We can do it because Jesus will do it through us.

[15] http://www.studylight.org/lexicons/greek, HELPS Lexicon, Greek Perfect.

[16] In the natural realm, the dying process can be sudden or drawn out, but it always ends at the point of death. Crucified victims often took some time to die, but death always came. The same is true spiritually. When Scripture talks of the death of the flesh, it is talking about death, not a constant state of dying. As part of the dying process we have a daily responsibility to repent, renounce, and war against the flesh. However, this only continues until God crucifies our selfish nature and brings it to the point of complete death.

[17] The work of God in setting people free from their sin is entirely a work of grace, and grace is only accessed by faith. Physical death is a physical event and technically a work for it takes no faith to physically die. As such, this teaching suggests that our works are greater than God's grace. In essence, this doctrine is a form of the salvation-by-works doctrine.

Scripture is clear that our works simply do not work. Only the cross can completely deliver us from our sinful nature and we can only access the grace of the cross through faith. No work, including physical death, could ever save a person from their sin.

[18] See Jeremiah 17:9 and Ezekiel 11:19-20. The unredeemed heart is desperately wicked. Our selfishness is deceitful. The flesh nature is pure evil and it is utterly unable to obey God. For this reason, in the Book of Ezekiel, God promises to remove our heart of stone and give us a tender, responsive heart. To say that the new heart God gives us is wicked is a deception in itself. God can only give good gifts, and He offers us His heart so that we can obey His command of wholehearted love. This is a heart that is glorious in His love.

[19] See James 3:2, Jude 24-25, 2 Peter 1:10. The book of James is written to a compromising and adulterous church. James called the people sinners and instructed them to cleanse their hands and purify their hearts. In this sense, James was confirming the fact that before we encounter the cleansing and purifying work of the blood in our hearts, we do stumble in many ways. However, having been purified from our sin, if we continue to grow in our unity with Jesus, we will "never stumble." Is this by our own power or works? Jude 24 shows that it is only God who can keep us from stumbling. It is only by depending on His power and grace that we can live without stumbling or sinning.

It is important to note that these verses do not mean that we are unable to ever sin again. Anyone can sin. Even Adam and Eve could sin. These verses simply state that sin is not inevitable. When we live in union with Jesus, God Himself is able to keep us from stumbling.

[20] See 1 Timothy 1:12-17. A study of the context in which he speaks shows that Paul thought of himself as the chief or foremost of sinners because he was "**formerly** a blasphemer, persecutor and insolent opponent [or violent aggressor]." In the same way, he considered himself to be the least of all apostles because he persecuted the church **before** coming to know Christ. His comments regarding his sinfulness were based on his life as Saul, before he came to faith in Christ and was set free from sin.

[21] In Matthew 6:12, Jesus does indeed teach us to pray each day that God would forgive our debts as we forgive those who are indebted to us. And what is our debt to one another? In Romans 13:8 we find that we owe one another a debt of love. In this prayer, Jesus is not suggesting that we must always sin every day, but that we need forgiveness when we miss opportunities to love other people or fail to love fully. Likewise, we also need to forgive those people who did not love us perfectly.

[22] See Romans 7:14-20. To suggest that all believers are "of the flesh, sold in bondage to sin" is to completely misread the book of Romans and misunderstand the entire

gospel. Jesus came to destroy our bondage to sin, not to sell us into bondage. He came to destroy the works of the enemy and set us free from the law of sin and death. And when Jesus sets us free, we are free indeed.

So how do we make sense of Romans 7? We need to read this passage in context. At the beginning of the chapter Paul calls people to die to the law in order to be united to Jesus. The whole book of Romans was written so that people would find freedom in Christ from the sin nature and from religious legalism (the Law). Romans 7 specifically focuses on the Law and its effect on the selfish nature. In it, Paul describes what it is like to live in legalism and the intense conflict that comes as the rules of legalism empower the selfish nature. The goal of this chapter is to show the futility and hopelessness of living in legalism. This sets the stage for chapter eight and the celebration of freedom from sin and legalism through faith in Christ.

[23] To answer this objection we need to look at the context of this verse.

1 John 1:5-10
This is the message we have heard from him and proclaim to you, that God is light, and in him is no darkness at all. If we say we have fellowship with him while we walk in darkness, we lie and do not practice the truth. But if we walk in the light, as he is in the light, we have fellowship with one another, and the blood of Jesus his Son cleanses us from all sin. If we say we have no sin, we deceive ourselves, and the truth is not in us. If we confess our sins, he is faithful and just to forgive us our sins and to cleanse us from all unrighteousness. If we say we have not sinned, we make him a liar, and his word is not in us.

Let us look at the context. In verse seven and nine we see that the blood of Jesus cleanses us from all sin, and all unrighteousness. The natural result of being cleansed from all sin is to no longer have any sin.

Verse ten reads: if we say that we have not sinned. This points to the fact that people who have sinned in the past, possess sin in the present. This verse, when put together with verse seven, adds clarity to verse eight. Having sinned in the past, we have sin in the present, until the blood of Jesus cleanses us from all sin. But if we deny the presence of sin within us, we deceive ourselves. This deception keeps us from confessing our sin and experiencing the power of the blood to cleanse us from all sin.

There are many worldviews that deny the reality of sin and selfishness. It is common in the New Age to reject all moral judgments and distort the teachings of Christ by saying that there is no sin at all; there are only choices. They ask the question: How we can judge something as evil if it creates the conditions for good to be seen? For example, how can we judge the act of enslavement or torture as evil if it allows the victim to experience the beauty of forgiveness? And if such good can come from an evil action, is not the evil action itself ultimately good?

This kind of teaching is a deceptive attempt to justify the selfishness that lies at the heart of the New Age. The truth is that if we say that we have no sin and that we do not need the power of Christ's blood then we are deceived. We are all inherently selfish. We have all sinned and we all need His blood to be set free from sin. When we come into the light and let God expose the evil of our selfish nature, we will find that the blood of Jesus can wash away all our sin and conquer our selfish nature.

[24] See Proverbs 20:9, Psalm 24:3-4. It is true that apart from God, we are completely unable to cleanse our own sin or purify our hearts. God alone can do this work and He wants to flood us with the blood of Jesus that cleanses us from all sin. Blessed are those who have clean hands and a pure heart, for they shall stand in the Holy Place. Such people will not claim they cleansed their own heart, but will give all credit to the Lamb.

[25] Hebrews 4:15

[26] On the contrary, babies can be perfect or complete at their stage of maturity but still have a lifetime of growth and change before them. In the same way, we will always be able to grow in our unity with Jesus, who will always be our only perfection.

[27] *Sermons,* John Wesley, Vol. ii., p. 168.

12. Everything Already

[1] Perhaps unfortunately, most Bibles versions translate the aorist in Romans 6 to the past tense, however, others such as the King James Version, use the English present tense, reading:

> **Romans 6:6** (KJV, emphasis added)
> Knowing this, that **our old man is crucified with him**, that the body of sin might be destroyed, that henceforth we should not serve sin.

We must be careful therefore not to assume that because a statement is written in the past tense in our English bibles, that it is already true for all believers, regardless of faith or maturity. The reality is that if we want to experience the circumcision of the heart, we need to have faith specifically for our spiritual circumcision in Christ.

2   In this sense, our design of love is like a gift within a gift. In order to enjoy the gift of wholehearted love, we must first open the gift of a circumcised heart. Many people are seeking love, but when they pick up the gift of circumcision, they read the tag and reject it, not realising the treasure it contains. Most often, people reject it because it offends their theology. Some are afraid. Some people cannot bear the thought of loving God with all their wealth. Others are deceived. But there are people who dare to open the gift of circumcision. These ones find their lives forever changed by the glory of God's consuming love. Be one of those people. Be strong and courageous. Open the gift.

3   This is essentially a Christian form of a New Age teaching. The New Age promotes the law of attraction, namely that what we intently focus on becomes our reality. If we focus on wealth, we attract wealth. If we focus on success, we attract success. Yet this is not without its consequences. Remember that the spirit realm works through agreement. When a person engages in creative belief, they make an agreement with a spirit, which then acts to fulfil that belief. To the person it seems miraculous—"I just started focusing on wealth and the same day I found $100!" But it comes at a price: a demonic bondage. The spirit guides of the New Age are not there to serve people but to enslave them. They promise to help people become "masters," but their only goal is to master people. If you have been involved in the New Age, practicing the law of attraction, or have been engaging with spirit guides, break off your agreements and send them away. Call on the blood of Jesus to completely cleanse you.

The Christian teaching that belief creates reality substitutes faith in God with self-generated belief. Instead of listening to what He wants and working with Him to bring His will into reality, this teaching allows us to focus intently on our religious but selfish desires. We must focus on one thing: Jesus! As we focus on Him, we will naturally put His will first. And what is His will? That we would love God with our entire being and become one with Him. When we are united with Jesus, we can work with Him to bring His love into reality and so change the world!

14. Not I but Christ
[1] Psalm 119:41

15. Set Apart
[1] Elwell, Walter A. *Evangelical Dictionary of Biblical Theology*. Grand Rapids, Mich: Baker Books, 1996; *Sanctification*
[2] See Ephesians 4:24, Genesis 1:26
[3] *The Cost of Discipleship*, Dietrich Bonhoeffer, MacMillan (1959), p99
[4] Note that God took each one of us in that small group into a unique experience of the cross, which gave us a unique testimony to share with others. God will take you on your own journey to the cross and it may look incredibly different to mine or that of others. Simply open your heart to let the Spirit lead you in a way that is perfectly suited to you.

16. Righteous Judgment
[1] Psalm 11:6, 75:8, Isaiah 51:17,22, Revelation 14:10, 16:19
[2] Note that this verse says that "the wrath of God is revealed from heaven against all ungodliness and unrighteousness *of* men." It is the ungodly nature of the flesh that is the focus of God's wrath.
[3] John 3:13-15, Numbers 21:4-9
[4] See also Isaiah 33:11-12; Isaiah 29:5-6, Obadiah 18, Jeremiah 21:12, Genesis 19:24, Numbers 11:1-3

17. Immersed in Fire
[1] Luke 3:3
[2] Romans 8:4
[3] Daniel 3

18. Judgment and Design
[1] It is interesting that many people cannot believe that a loving God will judge people and send some to hell and others to heaven. But the same people will see a broken clock, a cracked cup, or a ripped shirt, and they will throw it away. Every day they will make judgments based on design and never question their own character. People argue against God's judgment not because they do not think that judgment is loving, but because they do not want to believe they will one day be held to account for their lives.

[2] 1 John 3:16-18

19. Renewing the Mind
[1] It is noted that linguistically the aorist includes aspect and not simply tense.
[2] Deuteronomy 11:18, Joshua 1:7-8
[3] Ideally, all inner-healing ministries should start with the design of love and the promise of a circumcised heart. Once the sinful nature has been removed by God, true healing of the heart and mind can then take place.

20. Blessing or Curse?
[1] The realm of blessing and curse is still relevant for all believers today. Like the Galatian believers, we can drift back into legalism and back under the curse (Galatians 3:1-14). Or like the believers in Rome, we can live according to the flesh and still experience death (Romans 8:1-17). It is important therefore to understand the nature of blessing and curse in Scripture.
[2] Deuteronomy 28:47
[3] Isaiah 5:20
[4] https://www.nature.com/articles/nn.3594
[5] This tuning is technically known as *methylation* of the DNA.
[6] 30 people = 2 parents + 4 grandparents + 8 great-grandparents + 16 great-great-grandparents. Note that only the effects of sinful experiences that occur before conception would be biologically inherited by the next generation. The effects of experiences that occur after the next generation are born would be passed on to that generation through relationship rather than biology.
[7] Philippians 2:13
[8] 2 Corinthians 5:21

21. The Fight of Faith
[1] I believe this observation was first recorded in *The Art of War* by Sun Tzu.
[2] I suspect that this is how Jesus suffered through every temptation. Imagine every type of demonic spirit projecting thoughts and feelings of lust, pride, greed, rage, onto Christ. Jesus would have felt these things, but He did not give into the feelings. He overcame every temptation, and now He can truly sympathise with us (Hebrews 4:14-16).
[3] For more on recognising the source of our thoughts and feelings, see *First Love*, Chapter 12, *The Source of Thoughts*.

⁴ It is important to note that when we lack sleep, we lose perspective and become particularly vulnerable to the arguments of the enemy. Whenever possible, we should avoid engaging with the enemy on a logical or emotional level if we are exhausted. We need to remember: sleep is a weapon. When we let our bodies physically rest, we refresh our brains, regain perspective, and can fight from a place of faith.

⁵ I remember once having to deal with a series of lustful thoughts. I took the thoughts captive but they kept on coming. Then I began to struggle with doubt. Had the enemy managed to re-sow lust into my heart?

At that time, a friend asked the Lord for a blessing to give us. God simply showed him a picture of a snake, rearing up and striking relentlessly. God then confirmed His word and our friend shared it with us. "I think you are in the midst of a relentless attack of the enemy. But God is saying to cut the head off the snake." I realised that this was an attack on my identity. I had been taking the thoughts captive, but not dealing properly with the source of the attack. *In Jesus name, I break every agreement with lust, I cancel this assignment against me, and through the blood of Jesus and the victory of the cross, I cut the head off this spirit.* Instantly the attack ended and the lustful thoughts ceased.

⁶ Note that there are only two sources of temptation: internal from the flesh nature or external from the world and the enemy. And they can feel almost the same but are dealt with quite differently.

James 1:14-15 focuses on internal temptation by saying that each person is tempted when they are lured by their own desires. Hebrews 4:15 speaks of external temptation when it says that Jesus was tempted in every way. We know that none of these temptations came from Jesus' own heart, but they all carried the same intensity that we experience, which is why Jesus can empathise with us. It is a mistake to think that because James speaks of temptation coming from the heart that all temptation comes from the heart. James is writing to double-minded (literally "doubled-souled") people. They have not yet experienced the reality of being crucified with Christ and so their own carnal desires are a source of ongoing temptation. Yet for those people who have been circumcised in their hearts, temptation is entirely external and needs to be dealt with as an external attack.

⁷ At times, the enemy may withdraw the sense of discouragement when we start striving to make us feel like we are overcoming in our own strength. This then leads us into the bondage of pride. Pride makes us feel like we are doing well, but it causes

us to ignore any lack of intimacy with God. We start to live for Him rather than with Him and so drift from our unity with Jesus.

8 Luke 5:29-32, 19:10, Romans 5:6-8

9 Note that there is a place for working through doubts or questions with the Lord. He wants to hear the questions of our hearts. God loves honesty and so, *"Lord, why did you let this happen?"* is a cry that the Father wants to hear. Processing genuine questions of our own heart will always lead to us into a deeper intimacy with of God and a stronger faith in Him. Conversely, dwelling on the doubts that the enemy shares with us will always be negative and will draw us away from God. So in order to discern the source of our questions, we need to look at where they are leading. If a thought is leading us on a downward spiral away from God, we need to take it captive and cast it out. If a thought is leading us to Him, then we need to follow it and let it produce as much intimacy with God as possible.

10 After I was crucified with Christ, the Spirit of God gave me 12 independent confirmations that the work was done. And I needed them. For me, these confirmations were like the 12 stones that Joshua set up as a memorial after they had come through the Jordan (Joshua 4:1-7).

11 1 Corinthians 10:13

12 Trusting in tears to support our case for forgiveness is a dressed-up form of unbelief in the infinitely good nature of God. He forgives us, not because we are distraught over sin, but because He is good, He loves us and He wants to be one with us.

22. All Authority

1 Colossians 2:11-15

2 In 1 Corinthians 3, Paul says that he could not write to the believers in Corinth as spiritual people "but as worldly people, as infants in Christ." The Corinthian believers were living in the flesh and were dominated by their natural senses. Because they had not yet been crucified with Christ, their conscious experience of life was being constantly shaped by the natural world more than the reality found in the spiritual realm. This focus on the natural world kept the believers in a state of spiritual infancy, unaware of their unity with Jesus.

3 Note that often people will ignore what they sense in the spirit because of the perceived awkwardness of dealing with a situation on a spiritual level. I had this in a Bible study once. The word did not seem to be penetrating people's hearts. There was a block, but because we were already into the flow of the study, it felt awkward to stop the study and pray. I stumbled along with the study for a while and then

finally stopped. We took a few moments to pray and we bound a religious spirit. Instantly the dynamic of the group changed. It was like a veil had been lifted and people started to engage with the word of God. Though it may be awkward, the fruit of freedom will always be worth the short time it takes to assert our authority in Christ.

[4] Not their real names.
[5] See 1 Corinthians 3:1-3
[6] See 2 Corinthians 4:1-4, Colossians 1:15-17, Hebrews 1:1-3

23. Overpowering Principalities

[1] See HELPS Word Study #3870. The word *parakaleo*, combines *para* ("from close-beside") and *kaleo* ("to call"). In various contexts it means to exhort, admonish, build-up, urge, and comfort from close-beside. This closeness is found in intimate relationship. When we form loving relationships, we open our hearts to receive true encouragement and correction as we spur each other on to love.

[2] As we saw in *First Love*, we can be a part of multiple groups of two or three, and these groups can overlap and evolve as the Spirit leads. Teams can then meet together with other teams and become home groups or house churches. These can then come together as assemblies. Our combined strength will enable us to fight greater battles and overcome greater forces of darkness.

[3] Psalm 133

25. Into the Land

[1] Romans 6:17, Ephesians 2:1-3
[2] Song of Solomon 8:5
[3] Deuteronomy 12:31
[4] Hebrews 12:16

26. Choose Life

[1] HELPS Word Study #7c (SN 2617a)
[2] 1 Corinthians 15:10

Small Groups

[1] The first four questions have been taken from John Wesley's guidelines for small groups.

One With Christ

onewithchrist.org

Made in United States
North Haven, CT
30 November 2023